COOKIE JAR

ALSO BY MARIA BRUSCINO SANCHEZ

Sweet Maria's Italian Desserts

Sweet Maria's Cake Kitchen

Sweet Maria's Italian Cookie Tray

SWEET MARIA'S

COOKIE JAR

100 Favorite, Essential Recipes for
Everyone Who Loves Cookies

MARIA BRUSCINO SANCHEZ

Illustrations by Dorothy Reinhardt

ST. MARTIN'S GRIFFIN ✹ NEW YORK

ISBN 0-312-28495-0

10   9   8   7   6   5   4   3   2

FOR THE

SWEET MARIA STAFF,

WHO CONTINUE TO INSPIRE ME THROUGH THEIR

INSIGHT, HARD WORK, AND SENSE OF HUMOR.

CONTENTS

ACKNOWLEDGMENTS

Thanks to my agent, Carla Glasser, for her dedication, enthusiasm, and for finally experiencing a mother-daughter cookie swap.

A huge thanks for my editor, Marian Lizzi, for again bringing her expertise and honesty to this, our fourth book together.

Everyone at St. Martin's, including Amelie Littell, Jennifer Reeve, Merrill Bergenfeld, and Michael Storrings, as well as Dorothy Reinhardt and photographer Anthony Loew for their tireless effort on my behalf.

As always, Mom and Dad for just about everything.

To Edgar, for being not only my encouraging husband, but a part of the Sweet Maria staff.

The Sweet Maria Staff: Aunt Dolly Mastronunzio, Aunt Babe DelGobbo, Lynn D'Aniello, Sarah Figluizzi, Maryse LeBlanc, Kaleen Overbaugh, Diana Ranganadan, Susan Tropasso, Sondra Tucci.

Thanks to my loyal customers who continue to challenge and support me.

Special thanks for sharing recipes: Mom, Aunt Babe Briotti, Sue Barron, Tom Butcher, Lynn D'Aniello, Richard Lee, Sandy Trusiewicz, and Betsy Walsh.

INTRODUCTION

Everyone loves cookies. From simple shortbreads to elegant linzers, cookies are a sweet treat that everyone enjoys. Each of us has our own personal favorite to eat and to bake. Every culture and family likes them. Whether enjoyed as a snack or dessert, or part of a simple breakfast, cookies have found a special place in our lives. I've never met a person who didn't like a cookie. For me, it's always difficult to choose a favorite. Cookies are as multiple as your moods. I adore a plain shortbread or ladyfinger along with a scoop of ice cream, a hearty biscotti as an after-dinner treat with an espresso, or a chewy chocolate chip cookie with a glass of cold milk for breakfast. When I was a kid, the cookie jar was always filled with something good, and that has never changed.

Cookies are also delightfully easy to make. They're not as intimidating or as fussy as cakes or breads. When I was growing up, cookie baking was a favorite hobby. I remember coming home from school, doing homework, and asking my Mom, "What kind should we bake tonight?" She would dutifully go to the refrigerator and take out several sticks of butter. The butter would come to room temperature while we ate supper, we'd clean the dinner mess, and then make a fresh batch. As I got older, I still found baking a relaxing hobby, even after getting a part-time job in a bakery. And it is really still a passion, although it has become my business for the last eleven years. There's nothing like rolling your sleeves up, getting flour on your nose, and eating a bit of cookie dough while you prepare a batch of cookies. Plus, when all the work is done, you have a delicious morsel or two (or more!).

Most of the cookies in this book are ones we bake at Sweet Maria's, my specialty cake and cookie shop. We bake about thirty-five flavors of cakes and about 20 (and growing!) types of cookies. We are committed to using the same fine ingredients that you use at home, although we bake in larger quantities. Fresh butter, spices, and extracts are essential for any size batch of cookies.

We've recently added an in-store cookie jar at the bakery, which we fill with the "cookie of the day." This sparks our creativity in creating new flavors and getting instant feedback on our creations from our customers. Many of the recipes here are the stars of that cookie jar.

This book is organized into sections that include All-American Cookies, International Favorites, Bakery Favorites, Chocolate Cookies and Simple Candies, Holiday Favorites, and Low-Fat, Low-Sugar, and Gluten-Free Cookies. There is also an index that organizes the cookies according to method, such as drop cookies, bar cookies, and rolled and filled cookies.

You'll find some of my family cookie recipes—some classics, others new variations of familiar favorites. With so many great cookies in the world, I've tried to give a broad selection. I've asked some of my friends to contribute their favorites and they were more than happy to share. Even customers will bring me their own cookies to show off their baking talents and family traditions. That's where the fun begins—sharing recipes and cookies. Sharing the cookies has also led to the phenomenon known as "cookie swapping," which is a fun way to share your favorite cookies with your favorite friends.

I hope this collection will become a part of your traditions and will inspire more great cookies.

So soften some butter, roll up your sleeves, and keep your cookie jar filled at all times.

INGREDIENTS

The ingredients used in this cookbook are widely available. Here's a list of some of the basics you'll need.

Flour

Unless specified in an individual recipe, all of the cookies in this book can be made with unbleached flour or all-purpose flour. These flours are readily available and are perfect in taste and texture. Cake flour is lighter in texture and may be recommended in certain recipes for very light and delicate cookies such as madeleines and tuiles.

Sugar

The sugar recommended for these cookies is fine granulated sugar.

BROWN SUGAR: Many recipes use brown sugar, which is simply granulated sugar processed with molasses for a rich flavor. You can use either light or dark brown sugar, loosely packed.

CONFECTIONERS' SUGAR: Confectioners' sugar is also known as powdered sugar or icing sugar. It is graded according to its fineness. The most readily available are 6X and 10X. You can use either in these recipes.

Eggs

Whole, grade A large eggs work the best for the recipes in this book. If you need to separate eggs, it's easier to do when they're cold.

Butter

Unsalted butter is recommended for the fullest flavor and texture. For most recipes, the butter will need to be soft enough to blend with sugar and other ingredients. Butter should hold an imprint when pressed but still retain its shape.

Shortening

Some of these recipes call for shortening. All-purpose vegetable shortening will work fine. Shortening baking sticks are now available in most supermarkets. These sticks make measuring very easy.

Oil

Unless otherwise noted, vegetable oil is preferred for these recipes. It is especially recommended for frying cookies.

Chocolate

Always use the finest and freshest chocolate available. The recipes in this book use a wide variety of chocolate; white chocolate, dark chocolate, and semisweet chocolate are the most widely used and the most readily available.

Cocoa

Because of the processing technique used to make Dutch process cocoa, it provides the fullest flavor and color for baking. It has less acidity and a rich, reddish color.

Nuts

A large variety of nuts and nut sizes are used for these cookie recipes, including almonds, hazelnuts, walnuts, cashews, peanuts, pecans, pine nuts, and pistachios. Be sure your supply of nuts is fresh. If you have a large amount, you can store nuts in a plastic bag in the freezer.

To coarsely chop nuts, use a cutting board and a sharp, straight knife. For nuts that are finely ground, pulse until desired size in a food processor.

Baking Soda and Baking Powder

Be sure that both of these leaveners are fresh. Store separately in airtight containers for freshness.

Extracts and Liqueurs

Extracts and liqueurs are used to flavor many cookies. Pure extracts and name-brand liqueurs are the best for the fullest flavor. Imitation extracts and cheap liqueurs may be less expensive, but you'll really sacrifice flavor.

Spices

Spices such as ginger, cinnamon, and cloves are used in these recipes. Be sure that your supply is fresh.

Citrus Rind

Orange and lemon rinds are used for a zesty citrus taste. When grating the rind, use a grater or zester. Be sure to avoid the pith, the white, fleshy, bitter part of the fruit.

Cream Cheese/Sour Cream

Many of the cookies have cream cheese or sour cream in their doughs. These often provide a richness and moisture that makes the cookie tender and tasty.

Food Color

You can add food color to either cookie dough or frostings. I prefer paste food colors. These are concentrated, so you only need to use a small portion. They are available in a multitude of colors and last a long time, if properly covered. Liquid food color is okay, but it will add liquid to your cookie dough or frosting.

Decorating Sugars

Colored sugars or sanding sugars are great for sprinkling on cutout cookies before they're baked or after they're frosted. They come in many different colors and can be the same texture as granulated sugar or coarser, like kosher salt.

EQUIPMENT

Much of the equipment used to make cookies are items that most people already have in their kitchens. Items such as mixing bowls, cookie sheets, cooling racks, measuring cups and spoons, spatulas and saucepans are a sampling of what you'll need.

Cookie Sheets

Sturdy, firm, clean baking sheets are an absolute necessity for cookie baking. You may use traditional sheets or the "air cushion" variety. The air cushion cookie sheets make cookies that are light in color and chewy. For crispier cookies, use a traditional cookie sheet.

Rolling Pins

You can use a marble or wood rolling pin to roll out your doughs. The choice is a personal one; use the kind you are most comfortable with.

Measuring Cups

Metal or plastic nested measuring cups are best for dry ingredients. Scoop and level off. Heat-resistant glass measuring cups with pouring spouts work best for liquid ingredients.

Parchment Paper

We consistently use parchment paper to line our cookie trays. This eliminates greasing the pan. Not only does it keep cookies from sticking or burning, but it also makes cleanup easier.

Silpat Baking Mats

These heat-resistant silicone mats are used to line cookie sheets. They are used in place of parchment paper and are washable and reusable.

Electric Mixer

A stand-up model electric mixer is a great tool. You can use a hand-held mixer for many of these recipes, but the stand-up gives you greater flexibility and efficiency. While the butter is creaming with sugar, you can tackle another task, such as preparing cookie sheets or chopping nuts.

If you're using a hand-held mixer, you may need to hand-mix the final amounts of flour in some recipes. If dough becomes stiff, stir in flour with a spatula or wooden spoon.

Wire Cooling Racks

Wire cooling racks are the best way to cool cookies after removing from the oven. The wire rack allows cool air to circulate under the cookie sheet for even cooling. Wire cooling racks are also essential for frosting cookies: Place a wire cooling rack on a parchment-lined cookie sheet. Place frosted cookies on wire rack. Any excess frosting will drip onto the parchment. For easy cleanup, just discard the parchment.

Containers

Many of the recipes call for storing baked cookies in an airtight container at room temperature. You can use cookie tins or Tupperware-type sealable containers. If the cookies are not delicate, you can also store them in plastic bags.

GENERAL TYPES OF COOKIES AND TECHNIQUES

Drop Cookies

Drop cookies are one of the easiest types to make. You simply drop the dough from a teaspoon onto a parchment-lined cookie sheet. No fussy chilling, rolling, or forming is needed. Most drop cookies spread when baked to form the cookie. If the dough is sticky, you can dust your fingers lightly with additional flour.

Rolled and Filled Cookies

Some cookies need to be rolled out with a rolling pin and cut into shapes. For most of these cookies, it's easier to chill the dough before rolling. Lightly dust your surface and rolling pin with additional flour. Too much flour will cause the cookies to become tough. Cut and fill as recipe directs.

Molded Cookies

This dough is usually broken into pieces and rolled and shaped, by hand, into a ball or crescent. If the dough is sticky, lightly dust your fingers with additional flour.

Refrigerator Cookies

This type of cookie is also called "slice and bake." The dough is rolled into a cylinder, usually about 2 inches in diameter. The dough is wrapped in plastic wrap and refrigerated 2 to 3 hours, or overnight. Remove from the refrigerator and slice dough into ½-inch slices. Place on cookie sheet and bake. This is a great cookie to have in the refrigerator or freezer for last-minute fresh baked cookies. To keep refrigerator cookies from flattening on one side, cut filled cylinder and place in a tall drinking glass. This will allow the dough to keep a round side.

Piped Cookies

This technique refers to squeezing or "piping" the dough through a pastry bag or cookie gun to achieve the desired shape. Different decorating tips and cookie-gun attachments produce a variety of shapes.

Bar Cookies

Bar cookies are an easy cookie to make. Ingredients are spread or layered in a pan, similar to a brownie. Many of the bar cookies in this collection use standard pans that are readily available, either an 8 × 8 × 2-inch baking pan, a 13 × 9-inch baking pan, or 14 × 10-inch jellyroll pan, depending on what the recipe specifies.

Many bar cookies use the "baking blind" technique, popular for making tarts. After preparing the crust in the pan, the crust is baked without filling to avoid the bottom from being soggy and undercooked. The filling is then placed on top of the hot crust and returned to the oven for additional baking.

Sandwich Cookies

Most of the sandwich cookies in this book use a chill, roll, and cut method. Be sure to keep the dough you're *not* working with chilled. This will help to keep the sizes uniform as you roll the shapes. It will be easier to match pairs when making the sandwiches. To fill, spread filling on the underside of one of the cookies. Gently press partner cookie to adhere with filling. Allow to dry completely before storing.

Biscotti

Biscotti are Italian cookies that are baked twice. The dough is shaped into loaves and baked. The loaves are then cooled, and sliced diagonally into ½-inch slices. The slices are placed in a single layer on a cookie sheet and toasted again. This produces a crunchy, hearty biscuit, ideal for dunking.

No-Bake Cookies

These are cookies that do not require an oven. Some resemble candies. They are a nice, easy way to make a sweet treat or top off a cookie tray.

Fried Cookies

Some cookies such as Guava Empanadas and Italian Fried Cookies are cooked by frying in vegetable oil. Use hot oil, 375°F., and fry until golden. Drain on absorbent paper. Fried cookies are best when served immediately.

GENERAL BAKING DIRECTIONS AND TIPS

Oven Temperature

The first step to successful cookie baking is to know your oven temperature. Use an oven thermometer or have a repairman check the calibration. If you use the oven a lot, you probably know how it performs; you can then make temperature adjustments. If you don't bake a lot, check it before you begin. Just because your oven is new, don't assume the temperature is accurate.

Mixing Methods

CREAMING METHOD: This is the most popular method for making cookie dough, and many of the recipes in this book use it. You start with either butter, margarine, or shortening (whatever the recipe directs) and beat it in an electric mixer. Adding the sugar comes next. This is the important part of the creaming method. You must beat butter and sugar until light in color and fluffy. The butter must be at room temperature for proper creaming. Eggs are usually added next, then dry ingredients just until blended. Many popular cookies, like chocolate chip, oatmeal raisin, and brownies, require this method.

SPONGE METHOD: The sponge method is similar to the process for making a sponge cake. Egg whites are beaten until stiff. Separately, butter and sugar are creamed; egg yolks and dry ingredients are added to the butter-sugar mixture. The egg whites are gently folded into the butter mixture to make a delicate batter for cookies. One cookie that is mixed by using the sponge method is the madeleine.

Baking Times

Baking times included in these recipes are approximate. Directions are also given for what the finished cookie should look like. If a recipe says 10 to 12 minutes or until golden brown and you check after 12 minutes and the cookies are still not golden brown, bake an additional 1 to 2 minutes until proper color is achieved. Some ovens may bake unevenly. If your oven does, check the cookies halfway through the suggested baking time. You may need to rotate the cookie sheet for even baking.

I love an oven door with a light and a window. It allows you to check the baking progress without opening the oven door and letting out heat.

Chopping Nuts

Whole almonds and walnut halves are used in this book, usually as a garnish for the top of a cookie. These are readily available in most supermarkets. If you need coarsely chopped nuts, use a cutting board and a sharp, straight knife. Finely chopped nuts can be done in a food processor. A few quick pulses should do the trick.

Egg Wash

Egg wash is simply a bakery term for brushing the tops of cookies with a lightly beaten egg. This adds a shine and a professional look to some cookies.

Dusting or Rolling in Confectioners' Sugar

Many cookies in this book are finished with a dusting of confectioners' sugar, also known as powdered sugar. To dust cookies, place a few tablespoons of confectioners' sugar into a small strainer. Using a spoon, stir the sugar around the strainer while holding it over the cookies. Repeat as necessary.

To coat cookies in confectioners' sugar, place sugar in a medium bowl. Add 10 to 12 cookies at a time. Using your fingers, carefully toss cookies to coat, being careful not to break them.

Dipping and Decorating with Chocolate

TO MELT CHOCOLATE: I've always found the easiest way to melt chocolate is over simmering water in a double boiler. Be sure that the water is not boiling.

To melt a small amount of chocolate, you can also use the microwave. For 8 ounces chocolate, microwave 1 to 2 minutes on high.

If you're using chocolate for decorating, drizzling, or dipping, you may want to melt 1 tablespoon of vegetable shortening in every cup of chocolate. This will create a coating chocolate that will set without the work of tempering the chocolate.

TO DRIZZLE: Place the cookies close together. Dip a fork into melted chocolate. Swing fork back and forth over cookies to drizzle with chocolate.

TO DIP: Dip half the cookie into melted chocolate. Place on a parchment-lined cookie sheet. While chocolate is still wet, sprinkle with chopped nuts or candies, as desired.

Grating Citrus Rind

The rind of citrus fruit such as lemons, oranges, and limes is a great and natural way to flavor cookies. Use a zester or grater, and be careful not to use the white pith underneath.

Vanilla Sugar

Another way to flavor cookies is to use a vanilla bean. Using a small, sharp paring knife and cut the bean in half. Using the tip of the knife, scrape the inside of the bean into sugar, using the proportion of 1 bean to ½ cup sugar. You can use vanilla sugar, instead of plain sugar and vanilla extract, to flavor cookies.

Filling and Using a Pastry Bag

Some cookies are formed using a pastry bag. This will give you professional-looking cookies at home. Here's an easy way to fill the pastry bag. Place the empty bag, tip side down, into a tall drinking glass. Fold the edges over the rim of the glass. This will give you a steady, open bag. Spoon dough into bag, being careful not to overfill it. Gather up the edges and remove from the glass. To use, simply squeeze the center of the bag, releasing the dough from the bottom. Practice will help you regulate the sizes and shapes of whatever you're piping.

Figuring Cookie Quantities

It's always hard to guesstimate how many cookies you'll need for a particular event. If the cookies are being used as favors or take-home gifts, you'll need to have one large cookie for each guest. If they are fancy cookies on a tray, a safe guess is usually 4 to 5 cookies per person. If you're serving other desserts as well, you can probably figure 2 to 3 cookies per person.

Storage

The best way to store cookies for short periods of time is at room temperature in air-tight containers. Re-sealable containers like Tupperware are ideal. It is best to keep different types of cookies in separate storage bins. This way, each cookie can keep its own true flavor. If you need to store cookies for a longer period of time, freezing is the best way. Refrigeration is fine for making dough in advance, but not for baked cookies, which will become stale more quickly in the refrigerator.

Freezing Dough

Freezing cookie dough is a great way to work ahead if you're making a large quantity of cookies. Many of the butter-based doughs, especially refrigerator cookies, are ideal for freezing. You can even take a small portion from the freezer and bake it whenever you want a few fresh-baked cookies.

Freezing Baked Cookies

An easy way to freeze cookies that are already baked is to use heavy-duty freezer plastic bags. If you are freezing cookies that need icing or dusting in sugar, freeze without the icing. Then, remove from freezer, thaw, and frost as desired.

CHAPTER 1

ALL-AMERICAN COOKIES

The cookies in this chapter include perennial favorites such as chocolate chip and oatmeal raisin. You'll find classics as well as new variations. Considering that the United States is a melting pot, many different cultures influenced all of the food we now consider American, but somehow the results seem all our own.

From traditional toll house to oatmeal raisin, maple walnut, and peanut butter, these are the cookies we rely on for comfort. They're the perfect take-along treat for school lunches, picnics, and tailgate parties.

CHOCOLATE CHIP COOKIES

This classic cookie recipe just can't be beat. It's the perfect combination of butter and chocolate; the ultimate comfort food. I like them chewy, slightly undercooked. If you prefer crunchy cookies, bake 3 to 5 minutes longer.

If we ever overbake a batch of these cookies—or burn them—my cousin Steve is very happy. He loves his Chocolate Chip Cookies burnt.

1/2 POUND BUTTER, SOFTENED	1 TEASPOON BAKING SODA
3/4 CUP SUGAR	1/2 TEASPOON SALT
3/4 CUP BROWN SUGAR	2 1/2 CUPS CHOCOLATE CHIPS
1 TEASPOON VANILLA EXTRACT	1 CUP WALNUTS, COARSELY CHOPPED (OPTIONAL)
2 EGGS	
2 1/4 CUPS FLOUR	

1. Preheat oven to 350°F.

2. In an electric mixer, on medium speed, cream the butter, sugar, and brown sugar until light. Add vanilla and eggs. Mix until well blended.

3. On low speed, add flour, baking soda, and salt. Mix just until blended.

4. Stir in chocolate chips and nuts.

5. Drop dough from a teaspoon onto a parchment-lined cookie sheet, spacing cookies 2 inches apart.

6. Bake 10 to 12 minutes or until lightly browned.

7. Remove cookie sheet from the oven. Using a metal spatula, remove cookies from the cookie sheet and place on a wire cooling rack. Cool on wire racks. Store cookies in an airtight container.

YIELD: 50 COOKIES

Variation: White Chocolate Chip Cookies

This is a nice variation on the traditional toll house cookie. Substitute white chocolate chips for semisweet chocolate chips.

Variation: Large Cookies

Many people love a "mall-size" cookie. You can easily make them at home and use them to make ice cream sandwiches. Use an ice cream scoop to spoon dough onto a parchment-lined cookie sheet. Gently press the top of the cookie to flatten. Bake 12 to 15 minutes, or until lightly browned.

YIELD: 20 COOKIES

◆ "BIRTHDAY CAKE" COOKIES ◆

SOME PEOPLE LIKE TO DECORATE A COOKIE AS IF IT WERE A BIRTHDAY CAKE. THE BEST TYPE OF COOKIE FOR THIS TREAT IS A CHOCOLATE CHIP OR OATMEAL COOKIE. TO MAKE AN 8-INCH ROUND COOKIE, PLACE AN 8-INCH CAKE PAN ONTO A PARCHMENT-LINED COOKIE SHEET. TRACE THE OUTSIDE OF THE PAN WITH A PENCIL. TURN THE PARCHMENT OVER SO THAT THE PENCIL MARKS ARE ON THE UNDERSIDE. SCOOP COOKIE DOUGH INTO THE CIRCLE AND GENTLY PRESS TO FILL IN CIRCLE EVENLY WITH THE DOUGH. BAKE COOKIE UNTIL LIGHTLY BROWNED. YOU WILL NEED TO BAKE THIS A BIT LONGER THAN SMALLER COOKIES. LET COOKIE COOL COMPLETELY ON PARCHMENT PAPER. WHEN COOL, SLIP A DOILY-LINED CORRUGATED CAKE CIRCLE UNDER THE COOKIE. THIS WILL HELP TO SUPPORT THE COOKIE AND MAKES A NICE PRESENTATION. USE BUTTERCREAM FROSTING OR ROYAL ICING TO PIPE BORDERS AND WRITING ON COOKIE. CUT INTO WEDGES AND SERVE.

CHOCOLATE CHIP
ICE CREAM SANDWICHES

*These treats are the classic combination of chocolate chip
cookies and vanilla ice cream. Be sure to work quickly
so that your ice cream doesn't melt.*

20 LARGE (4-INCH-DIAMETER)
CHOCOLATE CHIP COOKIES
(SEE VARIATION, PREVIOUS
RECIPE)

ONE-HALF GALLON VANILLA ICE
CREAM

NUTS AND SPRINKLES (OPTIONAL)

1. Slightly soften ice cream in refrigerator. Place 1½ heaping scoops of ice cream
   onto the bottom of a cookie. Using a spatula, gently smooth ice cream to the
   edges of cookie. Press bottom of another cookie on top to form sandwich. Roll
   edges in nuts or sprinkles, if desired. Repeat until all cookies are filled.

2. Place sandwiches onto a plate or cookie sheet. Place in the freezer to harden.
   When firm, wrap each sandwich in plastic wrap or a cellophane bag. Store
   sandwiches individually wrapped in the freezer.

YIELD: 10 SANDWICHES

◆ ICE CREAM SANDWICHES ◆

COOKIES THAT HAVE A FLAT SIDE ARE THE BEST TO MAKE SANDWICHES.
HERE ARE A FEW OF MY FAVORITES:

COOKIE: CHOCOLATE NUTELLA COOKIE
FILLINGS: PISTACHIO ICE CREAM, COFFEE ICE CREAM, MINT CHOCOLATE-
CHIP ICE CREAM, PEANUT BUTTER OR RASPBERRY JAM
COOKIE: GINGERBREAD
FILLING: CINNAMON OR EGGNOG ICE CREAM
COOKIE: PEANUT BUTTER FORK COOKIES
FILLING: CHOCOLATE ICE CREAM, CHOCOLATE-CHIP ICE CREAM

OATMEAL CRUNCHIES

The finely chopped walnuts in this crunchy cookie
make this an ideal treat. It's one of the first
cookies I learned to bake and eat.

¼ POUND BUTTER, SOFTENED	1 CUP FLOUR
½ CUP SUGAR	½ TEASPOON BAKING POWDER
½ CUP BROWN SUGAR	½ TEASPOON BAKING SODA
1 TEASPOON VANILLA EXTRACT	PINCH OF SALT
1 EGG	¼ CUP CHOPPED WALNUTS
¾ CUP OATS	ADDITIONAL SUGAR FOR DIPPING

1. Preheat oven to 350°F.

2. In an electric mixer on medium speed, cream butter, sugar, and brown sugar until light. Add vanilla and egg. Mix until well blended.

3. On low speed, add oats, flour, baking powder, baking soda, and salt. Mix just until blended. Stir in walnuts.

4. Roll dough into 1-inch balls. Dip tops into additional sugar. Place onto a parchment-lined cookie sheet, spacing cookies 2 inches apart.

5. Bake 10 to 12 minutes or until light brown.

6. Remove cookie sheet from the oven. Using a metal spatula, remove cookies from the cookie sheet and place on a wire cooling rack. Cool cookies on wire rack. Store cookies in an airtight container.

YIELD: 36 COOKIES

OATMEAL RAISIN

This hearty cookie is a dig-your-teeth-into kind of cookie.
A chewy combination of butter, brown sugar, oats,
and raisins, they're good for you, too.

½ POUND BUTTER, SOFTENED	1 ½ CUPS FLOUR
1 CUP BROWN SUGAR	½ TEASPOON SALT
½ CUP SUGAR	1 TEASPOON BAKING POWDER
1 TEASPOON VANILLA EXTRACT	2 CUPS OATS
2 EGGS	1 CUP RAISINS

1. Preheat oven to 350°F.

2. In an electric mixer, cream butter, brown sugar, and sugar until light. Add vanilla and eggs. Mix until well blended. On low speed, add flour, salt, and baking powder. Add oats and raisins. Mix just until blended.

3. Drop cookies from a teaspoon onto a parchment-lined cookie sheet, spacing each 2 inches apart.

4. Bake 12 to 15 minutes or until lightly browned.

5. Remove cookie sheet from the oven. Using a metal spatula, remove cookies from the cookie sheet and place on a wire cooling rack. Cool completely. Store cookies in an airtight container.

YIELD: 50 COOKIES

CHOCOLATE CHOCOLATE CHIP COOKIES

*These double chocolate treats are the perfect treat for chocolate
lovers everywhere. They're great to enjoy on their own or
sandwiched together with your favorite ice cream. For
a variation, you can substitute white chocolate chips instead
of chocolate chips, for a white polka-dot cookie.*

2 1/2 STICKS BUTTER, SOFTENED	3/4 CUP COCOA
1 1/2 CUPS SUGAR	1/2 TEASPOON BAKING SODA
2 EGGS	1/2 TEASPOON SALT
2 CUPS FLOUR	2 CUPS CHOCOLATE CHIPS

1. Preheat oven to 350°F.

2. In an electric mixer, cream butter and sugar until light. Add eggs. Mix well. On low speed, add flour, cocoa, baking soda, and salt. Mix just until blended.

3. Stir in chocolate chips.

4. Drop from a teaspoon onto a parchment-lined cookie sheet, spacing each 2 inches apart.

5. Bake 12 to 15 minutes, or until firm. Remove cookie sheet from the oven. Cool cookies completely on parchment paper. Store in an airtight container.

YIELD: 60 COOKIES

PEANUT BUTTER FORK COOKIES

*Peanut butter is one of my favorite cookie ingredients. You can use
either chunky or smooth, depending on whether you want
a bit of crunch. They're called fork cookies because of
how you make the crisscross design on top.*

½ POUND BUTTER, SOFTENED	1 ½ CUPS CHUNKY PEANUT BUTTER
1 CUP BROWN SUGAR	2 CUPS FLOUR
½ CUP SUGAR	1 TEASPOON BAKING POWDER
2 EGGS	1 TEASPOON BAKING SODA

1. In an electric mixer, cream butter, brown sugar, and sugar until light. Add eggs and peanut butter. Mix until well blended.

2. On low speed, add flour, baking powder, and baking soda. Mix just until blended. Wrap dough in plastic wrap and refrigerate 4 to 5 hours or overnight.

3. Preheat oven to 375°F.

4. Roll dough into 1-inch balls. Place on a parchment-lined cookie sheet, spacing each 2 inches apart. Using your fingers, slightly flatten the tops. Dip a fork into additional flour. Press fork into the top of the cookies in a crisscross manner.

5. Bake 12 to 15 minutes or until lightly browned.

6. Remove cookie sheet from the oven. Using a metal spatula, remove cookies from the cookie sheet and place on a wire cooling rack. Cool completely. Store cookies at room temperature in an airtight container.

YIELD: 50 COOKIES

MAGIC BARS

These rich, layered bars have had many names over the years, including seven-layer bars and congo bars. Whatever you call them, they're a delicious combination of chocolate, coconut, walnuts, and sweetened condensed milk. For easier cutting, chill pan in refrigerator after baking.

¼ POUND BUTTER, MELTED AND COOLED

1½ CUPS GRAHAM CRACKER CRUMBS

1 CUP WALNUTS, COARSELY CHOPPED

1 CUP CHOCOLATE CHIPS

1½ CUPS FLAKED COCONUT

14 OUNCES SWEETENED CONDENSED MILK

1. Preheat oven to 350°F.

2. Place graham cracker crumbs in a small mixing bowl. Pour butter over crumbs. Mix well. Press into the bottom of an ungreased 13 × 9-inch baking pan. Sprinkle nuts evenly over crumbs. Sprinkle chocolate chips over nuts. Sprinkle 1 cup of the coconut over the chocolate chips.

3. With a tablespoon, drizzle the sweetened condensed milk evenly over the coconut. Sprinkle top with remaining ½ cup of coconut.

4. Bake 25 to 30 minutes or until lightly browned.

5. Remove baking pan from the oven. Cool in pan on a wire cooling rack. When completely cool, cut into squares. Store cookies in an airtight container.

YIELD: 24 COOKIES

SNICKERDOODLES

Simple and delicious, these cookies are rolled in a mixture of cinnamon and sugar. Since I was a child, the name has always been a mystery. Be careful not to overbake them; they should be slightly chewy.

½ POUND BUTTER, SOFTENED

1½ CUPS SUGAR

2 EGGS

2½ CUPS FLOUR

1 TEASPOON BAKING SODA

½ TEASPOON SALT

TOPPING:

4 TABLESPOONS SUGAR

2 TEASPOONS CINNAMON

1. Preheat oven to 350°F.

2. In an electric mixer, cream butter and sugar until light. Add eggs. Mix until well blended.

3. On low speed, add flour, baking soda, and salt. Mix just until blended.

4. In a small bowl, combine 4 tablespoons sugar and cinnamon.

5. Roll dough into 1-inch balls. Roll balls in cinnamon and sugar mixture. Place onto a parchment-lined cookie sheet, spacing each cookie 2 inches apart.

6. Bake 10 to 12 minutes or until firm.

7. Remove cookie sheet from the oven. Cool cookies completely on parchment. Store cookies in an airtight container.

YIELD: 48 COOKIES

BUTTERSCOTCH DROPS

These flavorful little drop cookies are sure to satisfy your
sweet tooth. They're loaded with butterscotch drops,
one of my mom's favorite ingredients.

¼ POUND BUTTER, SOFTENED	1 ½ CUPS FLOUR
1 CUP BROWN SUGAR	2 TEASPOONS BAKING POWDER
2 EGGS	¼ TEASPOON SALT
1 TEASPOON VANILLA EXTRACT	1 ½ CUPS BUTTERSCOTCH CHIPS

1. Preheat oven to 350°F.

2. In an electric mixer, cream butter and brown sugar until light. Add eggs and vanilla. Mix until well blended.

3. On low speed, add flour, baking powder, and salt. Mix just until blended. Stir in butterscotch chips.

4. Drop dough from a teaspoon onto a parchment-lined cookie sheet, spacing each 2 inches apart.

5. Bake 10 to 12 minutes or until golden.

6. Remove cookie sheet from the oven. Using a metal spatula, remove cookies from the cookie sheet and place on a wire cooling rack. Cool completely. Store cookies in an airtight container at room temperature.

YIELD: 36 COOKIES

MAPLE WALNUT DROPS

These moist and nutty drop cookies are the perfect autumn treat.
Serve them plain or with the sweet maple icing.

1 ½ STICKS BUTTER, SOFTENED

½ CUP SUGAR

½ CUP BROWN SUGAR

2 TEASPOONS MAPLE EXTRACT

¾ CUP APPLESAUCE

1 EGG

2 CUPS FLOUR

½ TEASPOON BAKING SODA

½ TEASPOON SALT

1 ½ CUPS WALNUTS, COARSELY CHOPPED

1. Preheat oven to 350°F.

2. In an electric mixer, cream butter, sugar, and brown sugar until light. Add maple extract, applesauce, and egg. Mix until well blended.

3. On low speed, add flour, baking soda, and salt. Mix just until blended. Stir in walnuts. Dough will be soft and slightly sticky.

4. Drop dough from a teaspoon onto a parchment-lined cookie sheet, spacing each 2 inches apart.

5. Bake 10 to 12 minutes or until edges are lightly browned and tops are firm.

6. Remove cookie sheet from the oven. Using a metal spatula, remove cookies from the sheet and place on a wire cooling rack. Cool completely.

7. Serve plain or frost with maple confectioners' icing (see page 25).

YIELD: 50 COOKIES

MAPLE CONFECTIONERS' ICING

3 CUPS CONFECTIONERS' SUGAR   ¼ CUP WATER

3 TEASPOONS MAPLE EXTRACT

In an electric mixer, combine all ingredients. Mix until well blended and smooth. Using a metal spatula, frost the tops of the cookies. Place cookies on wire cooling rack, with parchment paper underneath to catch any excess frosting. Dry completely.

◆ CRUNCHY VS. CHEWY ◆

FOR MANY DROP COOKIES, YOU HAVE THE OPTION OF BAKING CHEWY COOKIES OR CRISPY COOKIES. FOR CHEWY COOKIES, SLIGHTLY UNDER-COOK; FOR CRISPY COOKIES, SLIGHTLY OVERCOOK. WHICH IS BETTER? THIS HAS BEEN A CONTINUOUS SOURCE OF DEBATE FOR EVERYONE AT SWEET MARIA'S. IT IS REALLY A PERSONAL CHOICE, BUT I MUST SAY THAT I LOVE CHEWY CHOCOLATE CHIP COOKIES.

PEANUT BUTTER KISS COOKIES

*Proudly topped with a chocolate kiss, these cookies are
my friend and accountant Lori's favorite. I'm always sure to make
her a batch for her birthday—and for tax season! Just be sure to
press the kisses in while the cookies are still warm.*

¼ POUND BUTTER, SOFTENED	1½ CUPS FLOUR
½ CUP SUGAR	1 TEASPOON BAKING SODA
½ CUP BROWN SUGAR	½ TEASPOON SALT
1 TEASPOON VANILLA EXTRACT	ADDITIONAL SUGAR
1 EGG	30 CHOCOLATE KISS CANDIES
½ CUP PEANUT BUTTER	

1. Preheat oven to 350°F.

2. In an electric mixer, on medium speed, cream the butter, sugar, and brown sugar until light. Add vanilla, egg, and peanut butter. Mix until well blended.

3. On low speed, add flour, baking soda, and salt. Mix just until blended.

4. Roll dough into 1-inch balls. Roll in additional sugar. Place on a parchment-lined cookie sheet, spacing each cookie 2 inches apart.

5. Bake 12 to 15 minutes, or until golden.

6. Remove cookie sheet from the oven. While cookies are hot, press bottom of chocolate kiss into cookie. Using a metal spatula, remove cookies from cookie sheet and place on a wire cooling rack. Cool completely. Be sure chocolate kiss is firmly set before storage. Store cookies in an airtight container at room temperature.

YIELD: 30 COOKIES

PIÑA COLADA COOKIES

*Enjoy a taste of the tropics with these cookies. They're
a moist combination of pineapple, rum,
coconut, and macadamia nuts.*

1/4 POUND BUTTER, SOFTENED

1 CUP SUGAR

2 EGGS

2 TABLESPOONS RUM

2 CUPS FLOUR

1/4 TEASPOON BAKING SODA

1/4 TEASPOON SALT

1/2 CUP CRUSHED PINEAPPLE,
DRAINED

2/3 CUP FLAKED COCONUT

1 CUP MACADAMIA NUTS, COARSELY
CHOPPED

CONFECTIONERS' SUGAR FOR
DUSTING

1. Preheat oven to 350°F.

2. In an electric mixer, on medium speed, cream butter and sugar until light. Add eggs and rum. Mix well.

3. On low speed, add flour, baking soda, and salt. Mix just until blended. Stir in pineapple, coconut, and macadamia nuts.

4. Drop dough from a teaspoon onto a parchment-lined cookie sheet, spacing each 2 inches apart.

5. Bake 10 to 12 minutes or until lightly browned.

6. Remove cookie sheet from the oven. Using a metal spatula, remove cookies from the cookie sheet and place on a wire cooling rack. Cool completely.

7. Dust with confectioners' sugar. Store cookies in an airtight container.

YIELD: 50 COOKIES

CRANBERRY COBBLER BARS

These delicious bars are a quintessential New England dessert.
The cranberries and lemon give these bars the right amount
of zip. Try them plain or paired with a scoop
of fresh vanilla ice cream.

CRUST:

1½ CUPS FLOUR

1 CUP OATS

¾ CUP SUGAR

1½ STICKS BUTTER, MELTED AND COOLED

½ TEASPOON BAKING SODA

PINCH SALT

1 TEASPOON VANILLA EXTRACT

FILLING:

2 CUPS CRANBERRIES, FRESH OR FROZEN

GRATED RIND OF 1 LEMON

GRATED JUICE OF 1 LEMON

1. Preheat oven to 350°F.

2. In an electric mixer on low speed, combine all of the crust ingredients. Mixture will be crumbly.

3. Reserve one cup of crumb mixture. Press remaining crumb mixture into a greased 13 × 9-inch pan.

4. In a separate bowl, combine cranberries, lemon rind, and lemon juice. Spread over the top of crust mixture. Sprinkle cranberries with remaining crumb mixture.

5. Bake 30 to 35 minutes or until golden.

6. Remove pan from the oven. Place on a wire cooling rack. Cool completely. Cut into squares. Store bars in an airtight container.

YIELD: 24 SQUARES

GRANOLA COOKIE DROPS

These crunchy drops are a perfect breakfast cookie—tasty and not too sweet.
You can use store-bought granola or try our homemade recipe.

We first began making our own granola at Sweet Maria's several years ago.
It started as a way to use up a large inventory of nuts and oats.
The granola has now become so popular on its own, we never
have to worry about stocking too many nuts or oats!

1 CUP SUGAR	½ TEASPOON BAKING SODA
½ CUP VEGETABLE OIL	¼ TEASPOON SALT
⅓ CUP MOLASSES	2½ CUPS GRANOLA (SEE FOLLOWING RECIPE OR USE STORE-BOUGHT)
2 EGGS	
2 CUPS FLOUR	

1. Preheat oven to 350°F.

2. In an electric mixer on medium speed, mix sugar, oil, and molasses. Add eggs. Mix until well blended. On low speed, add flour, baking soda, and salt. Mix just until blended. Stir in granola.

3. Drop from a teaspoon onto a parchment-lined cookie sheet, spacing each cookie 2 inches apart.

4. Bake 10 to 12 minutes or until well browned.

5. Remove cookie sheet from the oven. Using a metal spatula, remove cookies from the sheet and place on a wire cooling rack. Cool completely. Store cookies at room temperature in an airtight container.

YIELD: 40 COOKIES

GRANOLA

You only need 2½ cups of granola for the cookies, but this granola is addictive, so you're sure to use the whole batch.

2 CUPS OATS

½ CUP RAISINS

¼ CUP ALMONDS, SLICED

½ CUP COCONUT

¼ CUP WHEAT GERM

¼ CUP VEGETABLE OIL

⅓ CUP HONEY

1. Preheat oven to 350°F.

2. In an electric mixer, combine oats, raisins, almonds, coconut, and wheat germ. Mix on low speed until blended. Add oil and honey. Mix until well blended.

3. Spread granola in a thin layer on a parchment-lined cookie sheet.

4. Bake 25 to 30 minutes, or until golden brown. With a wooden spoon, stir granola every ten minutes to cook evenly.

5. Remove cookie sheet from the oven. Let granola cool on cookie sheet. When cool, break up large bunches of granola. Store in an airtight container.

YIELD: 6 CUPS

KEY WEST LIME BARS

This variation of the classic lemon bar will make you pucker up.
I like them best chilled, served with a cup of espresso. You can
use either key limes or regular limes to make these bars.

CRUST:

1 1/4 CUPS FLOUR

1/4 CUP SUGAR

1/4 POUND BUTTER, SOFTENED

FILLING:

1/2 CUP SUGAR

2 TABLESPOONS FLOUR

1/2 TEASPOON BAKING POWDER

2 EGGS

1/4 CUP LIME JUICE (FROM 2 LIMES)

GRATED RIND OF 2 LIMES

CONFECTIONERS' SUGAR FOR
DUSTING

1. Grease an 8 × 8 × 2-inch baking dish. Set aside.

2. Preheat oven to 350°F.

3. Prepare crust. In an electric mixer on low speed, mix flour, sugar, and butter until the mixture resembles coarse crumbs. Press mixture into prepared pan.

4. Bake 12 to 15 minutes or until crust is lightly browned.

5. Prepare filling. In another mixing bowl, with wire whisk, mix together sugar, flour, and baking powder. Add eggs, lime juice, and lime rind. Mix until well blended. Pour mixture over hot crust.

6. Bake 10 to 12 minutes or until lightly browned and firm. Remove pan from the oven. Cool cookies completely in pan on a wire cooling rack. Cover and refrigerate overnight.

7. Dust the top with confectioners' sugar. Cover pan with plastic wrap and refrigerate. Cut into squares as needed. Serve chilled.

YIELD: 20 SQUARES

LYNN'S SUNSHINE
SOUR CREAM COOKIES

These moist little drops are a perfect treat when you need a little something sweet. They are tasty plain or with the orange confectioners' glaze.

1½ STICKS BUTTER, SOFTENED	JUICE OF 1 ORANGE
1 CUP SUGAR	1 CUP SOUR CREAM
2 EGGS	2½ CUPS FLOUR
GRATED RIND OF 1 ORANGE	2 TEASPOONS BAKING POWDER

1. Preheat oven to 375°F.

2. In an electric mixer, cream butter and sugar until light. Add eggs, orange rind, orange juice, and sour cream. Mix until well blended. On low speed, add flour and baking powder. Mix just until blended.

3. Drop dough from a teaspoon onto a parchment-lined cookie sheet, spacing each 2 inches apart.

4. Bake 10 to 12 minutes or until edges begin to brown.

5. Remove cookie sheet from the oven. Using a metal spatula, remove cookies from the cookie sheet and place on a wire cooling rack. Cool completely.

6. If desired, frost with orange confectioners' glaze or serve plain. Store cookies in an airtight container.

YIELD: 50 COOKIES

ORANGE CONFECTIONERS' GLAZE

See page 60 for Confectioners' Icing. Replace water with equal amount of orange juice.

FLUFFER NUTTER BARS

Named for everyone's favorite sandwich of peanut butter and marshmallow fluff, this bar has a flavor-packed peanut butter crust topped with fluff, peanuts, and chocolate chips. To help spread the fluff, dip your knife or spatula in water.

CRUST:

¼ POUND BUTTER, SOFTENED

1 CUP SUGAR

½ CUP PEANUT BUTTER

1 EGG

1¼ CUPS FLOUR

2 TEASPOONS BAKING POWDER

½ TEASPOON SALT

TOPPING:

2 CUPS MARSHMALLOW FLUFF

1 CUP PEANUTS

1 CUP SEMISWEET CHOCOLATE CHIPS

1. Preheat oven to 350°F.

2. Prepare crust. In an electric mixer, cream butter and sugar until light. Add peanut butter and egg. Mix until well blended. On low speed, add flour, baking powder, and salt. Mix just until blended. Press crust into the bottom and slightly up the sides of an ungreased 13 × 9-inch baking pan.

3. Spoon fluff over crust, spreading to cover. Sprinkle peanuts over fluff. Sprinkle chocolate chips over peanuts.

4. Bake 15 to 20 minutes or until top is lightly browned.

5. Remove pan from the oven. Place on a wire cooling rack. Cool completely. When cool, cut into squares.

YIELD: 24 SQUARES

BASIL CHEDDAR ROUNDS

You can use any kind of cheddar in these cookies but I like extra sharp.
These savory cookies are a perfect alternative to crackers, served
with your favorite soup. Or top with a dollop of pesto for
an easy make-ahead hors d'oeuvre.

¼ POUND BUTTER, SOFTENED

1 CUP SHREDDED CHEDDAR CHEESE

¾ CUP FLOUR

½ TEASPOON BAKING POWDER

½ TEASPOON SALT

2 TABLESPOONS FRESH BASIL, CHOPPED

1. Preheat oven to 350°F.

2. In an electric mixer, on medium speed, cream butter and cheddar until well blended. On low speed, add flour, baking powder, salt, and basil. Mix just until blended.

3. Roll dough out onto a lightly floured surface to ¼-inch thick. Using a 1½-inch round cookie cutter, cut into rounds. Place on a parchment-lined cookie sheet, spacing each 2 inches apart.

4. Bake 15 to 20 minutes or until edges begin to brown.

5. Remove cookie sheet from the oven. Using a metal spatula, remove cookies from the cookie sheet and place on a wire cooling rack. Cool completely. Store cookies refrigerated in an airtight container.

YIELD: 20 COOKIES

CHAPTER 2

INTERNATIONAL FAVORITES

The cookies in this section represent a small sampling from around the world. Many of these cookies began as a way to celebrate religious holidays and other special occasions, using the finest resources and ingredients. You'll find Cuban cookies that use the finest citrus and guava, gingerbread that uses the finest spices, and delicate madeleines that were developed by fine French culinary talents.

My grandparents are from Italy, so you will find a few Italian specialties in this section. If you'd like a more complete collection of Italian cookies, my first cookbook, *Sweet Maria's Italian Cookie Tray*, features many. This section also includes other favorites— almond cookies from Taiwan, shortbread from Scotland, and nut rolls from Eastern Europe, just to name a few. Many of my friends were happy to share their ethnic traditions and cookies that have become a part of their family celebrations. Try asking your friends to share, too.

RASPBERRY LINZERS

To make these classic Austrian sandwich cookies, you'll need a 2-inch round cookie cutter, plus a ½-inch cutter to make the inside cutout. The secret is to roll the dough thin and be sure to keep the dough you're not working with refrigerated. This will ensure that all the cookies remain the same size and will be easy to pair.

1½ STICKS BUTTER, SOFTENED

1 CUP SUGAR

2 EGGS

1 TEASPOON ALMOND EXTRACT

2¼ CUPS FLOUR

1 TEASPOON BAKING POWDER

½ TEASPOON SALT

CONFECTIONERS' SUGAR FOR DUSTING

FILLING

½ CUP RASPBERRY OR OTHER FLAVOR PRESERVES

1. In an electric mixer, cream butter and sugar until light. Add eggs and almond extract. Mix until blended. On low speed, add 2 cups flour, baking powder, and salt. Mix just until blended. Turn dough out onto a lightly floured surface. Knead in remaining ¼ cup flour to make a firm dough. Wrap dough in plastic wrap and refrigerate 2 to 3 hours or overnight.

2. Preheat oven to 350°F.

3. Roll dough out on a lightly floured surface to ⅛-inch thick. Using a 2-inch round fluted cookie cutter, cut dough into circles. Using a ½-inch round fluted cookie cutter, cut out the center of half of the circles. Re-roll and cut dough until you have an even number of bottoms (without hole) and tops (with hole). Place circles on a parchment-lined cookie sheet, spacing each 2 inches apart.

4. Bake 8 to 10 minutes or until edges just begin to brown.

5. Remove cookie sheet from the oven. Using a metal spatula, remove cookies from the cookie sheet and place on a wire cooling rack. Cool completely.

6. To assemble, pair cookies of similar size tops and bottoms. Dust tops with confectioners' sugar. Using a butter knife or small spatula, spread a small amount of preserves on the bottom cookie. Place a top over the preserves and press gently.

7. Dry completely. Store cookies in an airtight container.

YIELD: 36 COOKIES

SWEDISH SPICE COOKIES

Topped with a lemon glaze, these traditional Swedish spice cookies have just the right amount of spice. These are usually baked to celebrate Christmas.

1½ STICKS BUTTER, SOFTENED	½ TEASPOON SALT
¾ CUP SUGAR	½ TEASPOON BAKING SODA
1 EGG	½ TEASPOON NUTMEG
¼ CUP HONEY	1 TEASPOON CINNAMON
2 CUPS FLOUR	

1. Preheat oven to 350°F.

2. In an electric mixer, cream butter and sugar until light. Add egg and honey. Mix until well blended.

3. On low speed, add flour, salt, baking soda, nutmeg, and cinnamon. Mix just until blended.

4. Drop dough from a teaspoon onto a parchment-lined cookie sheet, spacing each 2 inches apart.

5. Bake 10 to 12 minutes or until light brown. Remove cookie sheet from the oven. Using a metal spatula, remove cookies from the sheet and place on a wire cooling rack. Cool completely.

6. Frost with lemon glaze. Store cookies in an airtight container.

YIELD: 35 COOKIES

LEMON GLAZE

1 CUP CONFECTIONERS' SUGAR　　　　**1 TEASPOON LEMON RIND**

2 TABLESPOONS WATER

In a small bowl, mix all ingredients. Lightly frost the top of each cookie. Dry completely.

BROWN SUGAR SHORTBREADS

*These simple sweet treats look great when you use a cookie stamp
to press down the tops. If you don't have a cookie stamp,
use a fork to make a crisscross design on top.*

½ POUND BUTTER, SOFTENED   1¾ TO 2 CUPS FLOUR

¾ CUP BROWN SUGAR   PINCH OF SALT

1. Preheat oven to 350°F.

2. In an electric mixer, cream butter and brown sugar until light. On low speed, add 1¾ cups flour and salt. Mix just until blended. Dough should be stiff enough to roll. If needed, add remaining ¼ cup flour.

3. Roll dough into 1-inch balls. Place on a parchment-lined cookie sheet, 2 inches apart. Use a cookie stamp or forks to flatten tops and imprint pattern.

4. Bake 12 to 15 minutes, or until lightly browned.

5. Remove cookie sheet from the oven. Using a metal spatula, remove cookies from the cookie sheet and place on a wire cooling rack. Cool completely. Store cookies at room temperature in an airtight container.

YIELD: 30 COOKIES

◆ COOKIE STAMPS ◆

COOKIE STAMPS ARE A UNIQUE WAY TO DECORATE COOKIES. THESE CERAMIC STAMPS, WITH RECESSED DETAILS, ARE PRESSED INTO THE COOKIE TO FLATTEN AND IMPRINT BEFORE BAKING. TO KEEP THE STAMP FROM STICKING TO THE COOKIE, LIGHTLY BRUSH IT WITH VEGETABLE OIL. COOKIE STAMPS WORK BEST WITH FIRM DOUGH LIKE SHORTBREAD. THEY ARE MADE IN VARIOUS DESIGNS AND CAN BE FOUND IN SPECIALTY KITCHEN SHOPS.

BRANDY SNAPS

These tasty, crispy cookies can be shaped into diplomas or cookie cups. They're easier to shape if you bake only 3 to 4 cookies at a time. Before shaping, let the cookies cool 1 to 2 minutes after removing the cookie sheet from the oven. Wrap the cookie around the handle of a wooden spoon to create a crispy cookie tube, or shape the cookie around the bottom of an upside ramekin to form a cookie cup. Fill them with whipped or ice cream for an impressive dessert.

¼ POUND BUTTER	½ CUP OATS
½ CUP BROWN SUGAR	½ CUP WALNUTS, FINELY CHOPPED
¼ CUP SUGAR	1 TABLESPOON HEAVY CREAM
½ CUP CORN SYRUP	1 TEASPOON BRANDY
⅔ CUP FLOUR	

1. Preheat oven to 350°F.

2. In a medium saucepan, over medium heat, combine butter, brown sugar, sugar, and corn syrup. Bring mixture to a boil, stirring constantly until sugars melt, about 3 minutes. Remove pan from the heat. Stir in flour, oats, walnuts, heavy cream, and brandy. Cool dough slightly.

3. Drop dough from a teaspoon onto a parchment-lined cookie sheet, spacing each 4 inches apart.

4. Bake until cookies are golden brown and bubbling has subsided, about 8 to 10 minutes. Remove cookie sheet from the oven. Let cookies cool 1 to 2 minutes.

5. Carefully shape cookie around the handle of a wooden spoon. Slide cookie off the handle and place onto a wire cooling rack. To form cookie cup, wrap hot cookie around the bottom of an upside-down ramekin. If cookies become too cool to shape, return pan to oven to reheat and shape. Cool completely. Store cookies in an airtight container.

YIELD: 30 COOKIES

ROYAL TEACAKES

These cookies have a great sconelike texture. It's the perfect match with a dollop of clotted cream and a spot of afternoon tea. When you use the cookie cutter to cut, you may get stuck cutting a raisin. That's okay—press on! Even the queen can't get enough of these casual, rustic, biscuitlike cookies.

4 TABLESPOONS BUTTER, SOFTENED	1 1/2 TEASPOONS BAKING POWDER
4 TABLESPOONS SHORTENING	1/4 TEASPOON SALT
3/4 CUP SUGAR	1 CUP RAISINS
1 EGG	1 EGG WHITE FOR TOPPING
1 1/2 CUPS FLOUR	ADDITIONAL SUGAR FOR TOPPING

1. In an electric mixer on medium speed, cream butter and shortening. Add sugar and cream until light. Add egg. Mix until well blended.

2. On low speed, add flour, baking powder, and salt. Mix just until blended. Stir in raisins.

3. Cover dough with plastic wrap and refrigerate 2 hours or overnight.

4. Preheat oven to 375°F.

5. On a lightly floured surface, roll dough out to 1/4-inch thickness. Using a 1 1/2-inch round cookie cutter, cut dough into circles. Reroll and cut until all dough is used.

6. Place rounds onto a parchment-lined cookie sheet, spacing each 2 inches apart.

7. In a small bowl, beat egg white with a fork. Brush the tops of each cookie with egg white and sprinkle tops with additional sugar.

8. Bake 10 to 12 minutes or until lightly browned.

9. Remove cookie sheet from the oven. Using a metal spatula, remove cookies from the cookie sheet and place on a wire cooling rack. Cool completely. Store cookies at room temperature in an airtight container.

YIELD: 36 COOKIES

HAZELNUT TUILES

*These cookies are the perfect way to impress your friends and family.
They are light, curved cookies that resemble roof tiles, or "tuile" in French.
They are beautiful on their own, or as an accompaniment for ice cream.
(You can even mold the dough into cookie cups for this purpose).*

*These cookies are best when baked on a lightly greased cookie sheet,
not on parchment paper. They need to cling to the cookie sheet. For
best results, bake only 4 to 5 cookies at a time. This will give you time to
shape the just-baked cookies before they cool. If they should cool before
you're done shaping them, return cookie sheet to the oven for 1 to 2
more minutes. Humidity can soften these cookies, so don't attempt
to bake these on a humid day. I've also found that using a cushioned
cookie sheet allows these cookies to bake more evenly.*

3 EGG WHITES	½ TEASPOON HAZELNUT LIQUEUR
¾ CUP SUGAR	½ CUP CAKE FLOUR
PINCH OF SALT	½ CUP HAZELNUTS, FINELY CHOPPED
¼ POUND BUTTER, MELTED AND COOLED	

1. Preheat oven to 375°F.

2. In an electric mixer, beat egg whites, sugar, and salt until thick. Add butter and liqueur. Mix until well blended.

3. On low speed, add flour and hazelnuts. Mix just until blended.

4. Drop from a tablespoon onto a greased cookie sheet, spacing each 5 inches apart. Using the back of the spoon, spread each into a thin circle.

5. Bake 10 to 12 minutes or until golden.

6. Remove pan from the oven. Using a metal spatula, carefully remove from the cookie sheet and lay on top of a rolling pin to form a curved cookie. (Shape on the bottom of an upside-down ramekin to form cookie cups). Cool completely. If cookies cool off before shaping, reheat cookie sheet in oven 1 to 2 minutes. Repeat with all the dough. Store cookies in an airtight container.

YIELD: 20 COOKIES

◆ HOW TO MAKE A COOKIE TRAY ◆

THE TRADITION OF MAKING COOKIE TRAYS FOR WEDDINGS, SHOWERS, AND HOLIDAYS IS STILL THRIVING. THESE TRAYS ARE A WAY TO SHOW APPRECIATION FOR THE BRIDE OR HOST. EVERY BAKER MAKES HIS OR HER SPECIALTY, AND THEY ARE POOLED TOGETHER TO MAKE LARGE TRAYS.

START WITH A FLAT TRAY OR PLATE. COVER IT WITH A DOILY, IF DESIRED. START LAYERING COOKIES, ARRANGING THEM FLAT ON THE TRAY. CONTINUE TO LAYER VARIOUS TYPES OF COOKIES, KEEPING THE FLAT, STURDY ONES ON THE BOTTOM AND THE LIGHTER, MORE DELICATE COOKIES ON TOP. BE SURE TO PAY ATTENTION TO COLOR, ALTERNATING ROWS OF CHOCOLATE, VANILLA, AND JELLY-FILLED COOKIES. WRAP IN FESTIVE CELLOPHANE AND RIBBONS.

MADELEINES

These delicate sponge cakes are light and sweetly flavored.
The method for making them is like making a sponge cake.
The key to success is to stiffly beat the egg whites and gently fold
them into the rest of the batter. You will need to use a
shell-shaped madeleine pan. These are available in most
kitchen stores. Madeleines do not have a long shelf life, so
bake and enjoy them as soon as possible. French
writer Marcel Proust would be proud!

1/4 POUND BUTTER, MELTED AND COOLED

1/2 CUP CONFECTIONERS' SUGAR

2 EGGS, SEPARATED

1 TABLESPOON GRAND MARNIER OR OTHER ORANGE LIQUEUR

2/3 CUP CAKE FLOUR

PINCH OF CREAM OF TARTAR

CONFECTIONERS' SUGAR FOR DUSTING

1. Preheat oven to 350°F.

2. In a medium bowl, with a wire whisk, blend butter and confectioners' sugar until smooth. Add egg yolks and Grand Marnier. Mix until well blended. Gradually stir in flour. Set aside.

3. In an electric mixer with wire attachment, beat egg whites and cream of tartar until stiff.

4. Fold egg whites into the butter and sugar mixture. Fold until well blended.

5. Spray madeleine pan with nonstick baking spray. Fill molds three-quarters full with batter.

6. Bake 10 to 12 minutes or until edges begin to brown and center of cookie springs back to the touch.

7. Remove pan from the oven. Carefully unmold cookies and place on a wire cooling rack. Brush out mold. Cool mold completely before re-spraying and filling. Repeat until all batter is used.

8. Dust cooled cookies with confectioners' sugar. Store cookies at room temperature in an airtight container.

YIELD: 15 MADELEINES

PALMIERS

*The rolled layers of dough in this classic French specialty resemble
palm leaves. This version, which uses cinnamon and sugar, is easy to
make if you use pre-made puff pastry. You can find sheets of frozen
puff pastry in just about every grocery store. Be sure to roll them on a
surface lightly dusted with granulated sugar. This sugar will work into
the dough as you roll and caramelize as the cookies bake.*

1 SHEET OF FROZEN PUFF PASTRY,
9 × 9 INCHES

½ CUP SUGAR

1 TEASPOON CINNAMON

1 EGG

1. Thaw puff pastry at room temperature for 20 minutes. On a lightly sugared surface, roll dough until thin into a rectangle measuring about 10 × 17 inches.

2. In a small bowl, combine sugar and cinnamon. In another small bowl, beat egg. With a pastry brush, brush the surface of the puff pastry with the egg. Sprinkle with cinnamon mixture to cover dough. Starting at opposite ends, roll up both sides of dough to meet in the center. Brush the outside of dough with remaining egg. Sprinkle with remaining cinnamon mixture. Place on a parchment-lined cookie sheet and refrigerate 30 minutes.

3. Preheat oven to 375°F.

4. Remove pastry from the refrigerator. Using a sharp, straight knife, cut dough into ¼-inch slices. Place cut side up on a parchment-lined cookie sheet, spacing each 3 inches apart. Bake 12 to 15 minutes, or until golden brown.

5. Remove cookie sheet from the oven. Using a metal spatula, remove cookies from the cookie sheet and place on wire cooling rack. Cool completely. Store in an airtight container.

YIELD: 24 COOKIES

RUGELACH

This traditional Jewish cookie is a rich and flavorful treat that was originally baked to celebrate Hannukah. These two versions are my favorites—raspberry almond and caramel chocolate chip. In this recipe, the dough is rolled thin into a circle like a pie crust, filled, cut into wedges, and rolled and shaped into a crescent.

CRUST:

½ POUND BUTTER, SOFTENED

1 EGG YOLK

¾ CUP SOUR CREAM

2 CUPS FLOUR

CARAMEL CHOCOLATE CHIP FILLING:

½ CUP CARAMEL ICE CREAM TOPPING

1 CUP WALNUTS, FINELY CHOPPED

½ CUP BROWN SUGAR

½ CUP CHOCOLATE CHIPS

RASPBERRY ALMOND FILLING:

1 CUP RASPBERRY PRESERVES

½ CUP SUGAR

1 CUP SLICED ALMONDS

1. Prepare crust. In an electric mixer, cream the butter. Add egg yolk and sour cream. Mix until well blended. On low speed, add flour. Mix just until blended. Turn dough out onto a lightly floured surface and knead until blended. Wrap dough in plastic wrap and refrigerate 2 to 3 hours or overnight.

2. Preheat oven to 375°F.

3. Divide dough in half. Leave unused portion of dough in refrigerator while you work with the first piece. Using a lightly floured rolling pin, roll out first half of dough until very thin, ⅛ inch thick, on a lightly floured surface.

4. Fill cookies. For caramel chocolate chip filling: Spread half the caramel ice cream topping over the dough. Sprinkle half the walnuts, brown sugar, and

chocolate chips over the caramel. For raspberry almond filling: Spread half the raspberry preserves over the dough. Sprinkle with half the sugar and sliced almonds.

5. Using a fluted pastry cutter, cut the circle into 16 wedges. Roll each wedge, starting at the wide end, toward the center of the circle. Pinch at the middle to adhere loose end of the dough. Slightly curve the cookie into a crescent shape and place seam-down on a parchment-lined cookie sheet, spacing each cookie about 2 inches apart. Repeat rolling and filling remaining dough.

6. Bake 15 to 20 minutes, or until lightly browned.

7. Remove the cookie sheet from the oven. Using a metal spatula, remove the cookies from the cookie sheet and place on a wire cooling rack. Cool completely. Store cooled cookies in an airtight container.

YIELD: 32 COOKIES

SLAVIC COLD DOUGH COOKIES

KIFFLES AND KOLACZI

*These Eastern European treats have a sweet yeast dough with a unique,
spongy texture. The nut rolls, or kiffles, are a favorite of my friend Tom.
His mom made these for all their family gatherings. Because the
dough is rolled out with a mixture of confectioners' sugar and flour,
you need to work quickly because the dough becomes sticky.*

CRUST:

1 PACKAGE YEAST

1/2 CUP WARM WATER

2 EGG YOLKS

2 CUPS FLOUR

1/4 POUND BUTTER, SOFTENED

2 EGG YOLKS

1/2 CUP SOUR CREAM

FILLING:

2 EGG WHITES

3/4 CUP SUGAR

1 1/4 CUP WALNUTS, CHOPPED

1 TEASPOON VANILLA EXTRACT

1. Dissolve yeast in warm water. Set aside.

2. Place flour in a food processor. Pulse in butter until mixture resembles coarse crumbs. Transfer to a medium bowl. Stir in egg yolks, sour cream, and yeast mixture. Turn dough out onto a lightly floured surface. Knead to make a soft, sticky dough. Divide dough into three equal pieces. Wrap in plastic wrap and refrigerate 2 to 3 hours or overnight.

3. Preheat oven to 375°F.

4. Beat egg whites until foamy. Gradually add sugar and beat until stiff. Stir in walnuts, and vanilla. Set aside.

5. Remove one-third of the dough from the refrigerator. Using a rolling pin dusted with a combination of confectioners' sugar and flour, roll dough out onto a surface that has been generously dusted with the same mixture. Roll dough very thin, like a pie crust.

6. Spread one-third of the filling on the dough. Using a pastry cutter, cut into wedges. Roll from the wide end to the center. Place on a parchment-lined cookie sheet, spacing each 2 inches apart. Be sure that seam is underneath cookie. Repeat rolling and filling remaining dough.

7. Bake 15 to 20 minutes or until well browned.

8. Remove cookie sheet from the oven. Using a metal spatula, remove cookies to a wire cooling rack to cool. Store in an airtight container.

YIELD: 45 COOKIES

VARIATION: KOLACZI

These jelly-filled rounds use the same tasty dough as the kiffles.

1 RECIPE SLAVIC COLD DOUGH
1 CUP RASPBERRY OR APRICOT JELLY

½ RECIPE CONFECTIONERS' ICING (SEE PAGE 60)

1. Prepare dough and refrigerate as directed. Remove one-third of the dough from the refrigerator. Using a rolling pin and board that has been dusted with a combination of confectioners' sugar and flour, roll dough out ¼ inch thick. Using a 2-inch cookie cutter, cut dough into rounds. Place on a parchment-lined cookie sheet, spacing each 2 inches apart. Cover top of cookie sheet with plastic wrap. Let cookies rest 15 to 20 minutes at room temperature. Using your fingers, make a well in the middle of each cookie. Fill with raspberry jelly.

2. Bake 12 to 15 minutes or until lightly browned. Remove cookie sheet from the oven. Using a metal spatula, remove cookies from the cookie sheet and place on a wire cooling rack. Cool completely. Drizzle tops of cookies with confectioners' icing. Let dry completely. Store cookies in an airtight container.

YIELD 30 COOKIES

CUBAN CITRUS COOKIES

These zesty cookies are a big buttery treat. Their refreshing flavor comes from a generous amount of citrus rind. You can use any type of citrus; I like a combination of lemon and lime.

½ POUND BUTTER, SOFTENED

1 CUP SUGAR

1 TABLESPOON GRATED CITRUS RIND

2 TABLESPOONS CITRUS JUICE

1¾ CUPS FLOUR

1 TEASPOON BAKING POWDER

¼ TEASPOON SALT

COARSE SANDING SUGAR TO DECORATE

1. Preheat oven to 350°F.

2. In an electric mixer, cream butter and sugar until light. Add rind and juice. Mix until well blended. On low speed, add flour, baking powder, and salt. Mix just until blended to form a stiff dough.

3. Roll dough into one-inch balls. Place on a parchment-lined cookie sheet, spacing each 2 inches apart. With the bottom of a glass, flatten cookies. Sprinkle with sanding sugar.

4. Bake 10 to 12 minutes or until edges begin to brown.

5. Remove cookie sheet from the oven. Using a metal spatula, remove cookies from the cookie sheet and place on a wire cooling rack. Cool completely. Store cookies at room temperature in an airtight container.

YIELD: 36 COOKIES

GUAVA EMPANADAS

These sweet Cuban turnovers can be either fried or baked.
The crust is a rich, flavorful dough made with cream cheese and
the filling is guava paste, which is a concentration of guava and sugar.
It is available in Spanish specialty shops and some supermarkets.
If you can't find guava paste, any tropical fruit preserve such
as pineapple or mango would be just as delicious.

CRUST:

¼ POUND BUTTER, SOFTENED

3 OUNCES CREAM CHEESE

1 CUP FLOUR

FILLING:

½ CUP GUAVA PASTE OR FRUIT PRESERVES

VEGETABLE OIL FOR FRYING

CONFECTIONERS' SUGAR FOR DUSTING

1. In an electric mixer, cream the butter and cream cheese until light. On low speed, add flour. Mix just until blended. Turn dough out onto a lightly floured surface. Knead to form a stiff, not sticky dough. Wrap in plastic wrap and refrigerate 2 to 3 hours or overnight.

2. Preheat oven to 350°F. (if you're not frying them). Remove dough from the refrigerator. Roll dough out onto a lightly floured surface about ⅛-inch thick. Cut into circles using a 3-inch round cookie cutter. Place ½ teaspoon of preserves in the center of each circle. Wet the edges of circle with water. Fold dough in half. Press edges together firmly to seal. Reroll, fill, and cut remaining dough. Let rest 15 to 20 minutes. For baking, place each cookie onto a parchment-lined cookie sheet, spacing each 2 inches apart.

3. Bake 15 to 20 minutes or until edges begin to brown.

4. Remove cookie sheet from the oven. Using a metal spatula, remove cookies from the cookie sheet and place on a wire cooling rack. Cool completely. Dust with confectioners' sugar. Store unused cookies in an airtight container.

5. For frying, fry cookies in hot oil, 375°F., until lightly browned. Drain on absorbent paper. Dust with confectioners' sugar. Serve immediately.

YIELD: 20 COOKIES

MEXICAN WEDDING CAKES

These buttery cookies are loaded with chopped hazelnuts.
They are traditionally baked to celebrate a wedding,
but I like to bake and enjoy them anytime.

½ POUND BUTTER, SOFTENED

⅓ CUP CONFECTIONERS' SUGAR

1 TEASPOON HAZELNUT LIQUEUR

1 ½ CUPS FLOUR

1 CUP HAZELNUTS, CHOPPED

CONFECTIONERS' SUGAR FOR DUSTING

1. Preheat oven to 350°F.

2. In an electric mixer, cream butter and confectioners' sugar until light. Add hazelnut liqueur. Mix until blended. On low speed, add flour and hazelnuts. Mix just until blended.

3. Roll dough into 1-inch balls. Place cookies on a parchment-lined cookie sheet, spacing each 2 inches apart.

4. Bake 10 to 12 minutes or until lightly browned.

5. Remove cookie sheet from the oven. While cookies are warm, toss to coat in confectioners' sugar. Cool completely. Store cookies in an airtight container.

YIELD: 50 COOKIES

CHINESE ALMOND COOKIES

These almond cookies are a traditional Chinese sweet. My friend Richard,
who is from Taiwan, bakes these as part of his childhood tradition.
The egg wash on top gives these cookies a professional look.

½ POUND BUTTER, SOFTENED	1 TEASPOON BAKING POWDER
1 CUP CONFECTIONERS' SUGAR	1 TEASPOON BAKING SODA
1 EGG	½ CUP ALMONDS, SLICED
1 TEASPOON ALMOND EXTRACT	WHOLE ALMONDS (ABOUT 40)
2 CUPS FLOUR	1 EGG FOR EGG WASH

1. Preheat oven to 350°F.

2. In an electric mixer on medium speed, cream butter and confectioners' sugar until light. Add egg and almond extract. Mix until well blended.

3. On low speed, add flour, baking powder, and baking soda. Mix just until blended. Stir in sliced almonds.

4. Roll dough into 1-inch balls. If dough is too sticky to roll, dust your fingers and the dough with additional flour. Place balls onto a parchment-lined cookie sheet, spacing each 2 inches apart. Using your fingers, flatten the tops of the balls. Press a whole almond into the center of each cookie.

5. In a small bowl, beat egg. Brush tops of cookies with egg.

6. Bake 10 to 12 minutes or until edges begin to brown.

7. Remove cookie sheet from the oven. Using a metal spatula, remove cookies from the cookie sheet and place on a wire cooling rack. Cool completely. Store cookies in an airtight container at room temperature.

YIELD: 40 COOKIES

SWEET WONTONS

These Asian-inspired fried cookies use wonton wrapper as a crispy crust to two simple fillings. These wrappers are available in most supermarkets. These are best served freshly fried.

CHOCOLATE CREAM CHEESE FILLING

8 OUNCES CREAM CHEESE

¼ CUP CONFECTIONERS' SUGAR

1 CUP CHOCOLATE CHIPS

1 EGG FOR ADHERING

25 WONTON WRAPPERS, SQUARE OR ROUND

VEGETABLE OIL FOR FRYING

1. In an electric mixer, cream cream cheese and confectioners' sugar until light. Stir in chocolate chips.

2. In a small bowl, beat egg. Fill wonton wrappers with ½ teaspoon of filling. Brush edges of wrapper with beaten egg. Press to seal edges. Fill all wrappers. Cover and refrigerate 1 to 2 hours.

3. Fry in hot oil, 375°F., until golden. Drain on absorbent paper. Dust with confectioners' sugar and serve warm.

YIELD: 25 COOKIES

VARIATION: TROPICAL FRUIT FILLING

½ CUP CHOPPED DRIED TROPICAL FRUIT (DRIED PAPAYA, PINEAPPLE, BANANAS)

½ CUP COCONUT

2 TABLESPOONS SUGAR

2 TABLESPOONS HEAVY CREAM

In a medium bowl, combine all ingredients. Fill wrappers and fry as directed above.

ITALIAN DROP COOKIES

ANGINETTI

This favorite, from my first cookbook, is the cookie that most people think of when they think of Italian cookies. They're very easy to make, and can be flavored with vanilla, anise, or traditional lemon. These are a "must have" on a Sweet Maria wedding cookie tray.

3 EGGS	1/2 CUP VEGETABLE OIL
1/2 CUP MILK	3 CUPS FLOUR
2 TEASPOONS LEMON EXTRACT	8 TEASPOONS BAKING POWDER
1/2 CUP SUGAR	

1. Preheat oven to 350°F.

2. In an electric mixer on medium speed, beat eggs, milk, lemon extract, sugar and oil until well blended.

3. On low speed, add flour and baking powder. Mix just until blended. The dough should be soft and sticky.

4. Using a teaspoon, drop the dough onto a lightly greased cookie sheet, spacing the cookies 2 inches apart.

5. Bake immediately for 8 to 10 minutes or until slightly browned.

6. Remove cookie sheet from the oven. Using a metal spatula, remove cookies from the cookie sheet and place on a wire cooling rack. Cool completely.

7. Frost with confectioners' icing (see page 60).

YIELD: 50 COOKIES

CONFECTIONERS' ICING

This versatile frosting is used for our Italian drop cookies and other recipes.
To make clean-up easier when frosting cookies, place a piece of
parchment paper under a wire cooling rack. Place frosted cookies
on the wire cooling rack. The excess frosting will drip
onto the paper, which you can simply discard.

6 CUPS CONFECTIONERS' SUGAR   **½ CUP WATER**

2 TEASPOONS LEMON EXTRACT

1. In an electric mixer, on medium speed, beat all ingredients until smooth.

2. Using a metal spatula, frost the tops of the cookies. The frosting will drip down the sides and coat the cookie.

3. Dry the frosted cookies on wire cooling racks. Store in an airtight container.

YIELD: ENOUGH FOR 50 COOKIES

PIGNOLI COOKIES

These almond macaroons covered in pine nuts, along with their chocolate almond variation, are so popular at the bakery, we can't seem to make them quick enough. This dough is a bit sticky, so try dipping your fingers in water as you roll it. This will keep the dough from sticking to your fingers and will help the nuts to adhere to the cookies.

1½ POUNDS ALMOND PASTE, BROKEN
INTO PEBBLE-SIZE PIECES

1½ CUPS SUGAR

1 CUP CONFECTIONERS' SUGAR

4 EGG WHITES

2 CUPS PINE NUTS

1. Preheat oven to 350°F.

2. In an electric mixer, combine almond paste, sugar, confectioners' sugar, and egg whites on low speed until blended. Mix on medium speed for 2 minutes. This will make a sticky dough.

3. Roll dough into 1-inch balls. Roll balls in a bowl of pine nuts, pressing to adhere the nuts. Place the cookies on a parchment-lined cookie sheet, spacing them 2 inches apart. Using your fingers, press to slightly flatten the tops of the cookies.

4. Bake 15 to 20 minutes, or until golden brown.

5. Remove the cookie sheet from the oven. For easiest removal, let cookies cool completely on parchment. When cookies are completely cool, use a metal spatula to loosen them from the parchment paper. Store in an airtight container.

YIELD: 50 COOKIES

Variation:

Chocolate Almond Macaroons

Bake these cookies alongside the pignoli nut cookies to check for doneness.

1 1/2 POUNDS ALMOND PASTE, BROKEN
INTO PEBBLE-SIZE PIECES

1/2 CUP COCOA

1 1/2 CUPS SUGAR

1 CUP CONFECTIONERS' SUGAR

4 EGG WHITES

2 CUPS ALMONDS, SLICED

1. Follow same directions as above for pignoli nut cookies. Add cocoa when you add sugars. Roll cookies in almonds instead of pine nuts.

AMARETTO BISCOTTI WITH ALMONDS

These biscotti, from my first cookbook, are the most popular ones we make. They're perfect with a hot cup of cappuccino. They are baked using the traditional method, first forming a loaf and baking, then slicing diagonally and toasting.

½ POUND BUTTER, SOFTENED	6 CUPS FLOUR
1½ CUPS SUGAR	2 CUPS SLICED ALMONDS
6 EGGS	6 TEASPOONS BAKING POWDER
2 TEASPOONS VANILLA EXTRACT	PINCH OF SALT
2 TABLESPOONS AMARETTO LIQUEUR	

1. Preheat oven to 350°F.

2. In an electric mixer, cream the butter and sugar until light. Add eggs, vanilla, and amaretto liqueur. Mix well.

3. On low speed, add flour, almonds, baking powder, and salt. Mix just until blended. Turn dough out onto a lightly floured surface. Divide dough into 5 equal pieces. Roll each piece into loaves about 12 inches long. Place on a parchment-lined cookie sheet, spacing each loaf about 2 inches apart.

4. Bake 20 to 25 minutes, or until well browned. Using 2 metal spatulas, carefully remove the loaves from the cookie sheet onto a wire cooling rack. Cool.

5. Place cooled loaves on a cutting board. Using a sharp knife, slice diagonally into ½-inch-wide strips. Place strips in a single layer on cookie sheet. Return to the oven for 12 to 15 minutes, or until lightly browned.

6. Remove cookie sheet from the oven. Cool toasted biscotti on a wire cooling rack. Store in an airtight container.

YIELD: 50 COOKIES

DRIED CHERRY AND ALMOND BISCOTTI

These biscotti are made in the traditional Italian style, without fat.
Because they don't have butter or any other type of fat, they harden
to a crunchy cookie. Be sure to slice them while they're still warm.

1 1/4 TO 1 3/4 CUPS FLOUR	1 CUP DRIED CHERRIES
1 CUP SUGAR	1 CUP WHOLE ALMONDS
2 TEASPOONS BAKING POWDER	3 EGGS
1/4 TEASPOON SALT	2 TEASPOONS AMARETTO
1 TEASPOON CINNAMON	

1. Preheat oven to 350°F.

2. In a large mixing bowl, combine 1¼ cups flour, sugar, baking powder, salt, cinnamon, cherries, and almonds. In a separate bowl, beat eggs with a wire whisk. Add amaretto and mix well.

3. Pour wet ingredients into dry ingredients. Mix to form a soft dough. Turn dough out onto a floured surface. If dough is sticky, knead in an additional ¼ to ½ cup of flour. Dough should be soft but not sticky.

4. Divide dough into 3 equal pieces. Roll each piece into a loaf about 12 inches long. Place on a parchment-lined cookie sheet, spacing each 4 inches apart.

5. Bake 20 to 25 minutes or until golden brown.

6. While cookies are still warm, slice diagonally into ½-inch slices. Return cookies to the cookie sheet in a single layer. Bake 15 minutes or until well toasted.

7. Remove cookie sheet from the oven. Using a metal spatula, remove cookies and place on a wire cooling rack. Cool. Store cookies in an airtight container.

YIELD: 30 BISCOTTI

ITALIAN LOVE KNOTS

TARALLI

*These classic Italian biscuits can be shaped into an s, a knot,
or a twist. I love to eat these plain, but you can
top them with confectioners' icing.*

½ POUND BUTTER, SOFTENED	½ TEASPOON VANILLA EXTRACT
¾ CUP SUGAR	2½ CUPS FLOUR
¼ CUP VEGETABLE OIL	2 TEASPOONS BAKING POWDER
4 EGGS	

1. Preheat oven to 350°F.

2. In an electric mixer, cream butter and sugar until light. Add oil, eggs, and vanilla. Mix well.

3. On low speed, add 2 cups of flour and baking powder. Mix just until blended. Turn dough out onto a lightly floured surface. Knead in remaining ½ cup of flour. Knead until the dough is soft but not sticky. Cover with plastic wrap and let dough rest at room temperature 15 to 20 minutes.

4. Break off pieces of dough and roll on a lightly floured surface into small snakes, about ½ inch wide by 4 inches long. Twist or knot dough pieces, or shape into an s. Place on a parchment-lined cookie sheet, spacing each 2 inches apart.

5. Bake 10 to 12 minutes or until edges begin to brown.

6. Remove cookie sheet from the oven. Using a metal spatula, remove cookies from the sheet and place on a wire cooling rack. Cool completely.

7. Frost, if desired, with confectioners' icing (see page 60). Store cookies in an airtight container.

YIELD: 36 COOKIES

ITALIAN FRIED COOKIES

CENCI

There are many versions of this type of fried cookie. Every family has their favorite way to flavor and shape these fried treats. This version is light and crispy but adds a touch of cinnamon. The secret to success is to roll the dough very thin and fry in very hot oil.

3 EGGS

1/4 CUP SUGAR

2 TABLESPOONS HEAVY CREAM

2 TABLESPOONS SHORTENING, MELTED AND COOLED

1 TEASPOON VANILLA EXTRACT

2 TO 2 1/2 CUPS FLOUR

1/2 TEASPOON SALT

1/2 TEASPOON CINNAMON

VEGETABLE OIL FOR FRYING

CONFECTIONERS' SUGAR FOR DUSTING

1. In a medium mixing bowl, whisk eggs and sugar. Add heavy cream, shortening, and vanilla. Mix until well blended. Add 2 cups flour, salt, and cinnamon. Turn dough out onto a lightly floured surface. Knead to make a soft dough. If dough is too sticky, add additional flour. Wrap dough in plastic and refrigerate 2 to 3 hours or overnight.

2. Divide dough in half. Roll dough out onto a lightly floured surface until very thin. Using a fluted pastry cutter, cut dough into various sizes of triangles. Repeat with remaining dough.

3. Fry in hot oil, 375°F., until well browned. Drain on absorbent paper. Dust with confectioners' sugar and serve. Store in an airtight container.

YIELD: ABOUT 40 TRIANGLES

GORGONZOLA PEPPER BISCUITS

These savory cookies use Italian blue cheese and black pepper, a great combination. You can use any type of blue cheese you like, but gorgonzola has always been a family favorite. Pair these biscuits with grapes and wine for an easy-to-prepare appetizer. Delicioso!

1 TO 1¼ CUPS FLOUR	1 CUP GORGONZOLA, CRUMBLED
2 TEASPOONS BLACK PEPPER	4 TABLESPOONS BUTTER, SOFTENED
1 CUP WALNUTS, FINELY CHOPPED	2 EGG YOLKS

1. In a medium bowl, combine 1 cup flour, black pepper and walnuts. Using a pastry blender, cut gorgonzola and butter into flour mixture. Mix until mixture resembles coarse crumbs.

2. Using a wooden spoon, add egg yolks. Turn dough out onto a lightly floured surface. Knead in additional ¼ cup of flour to make a stiff dough. Divide dough into thirds. Shape each piece into cylinders about 10 inches long. Wrap in plastic wrap and refrigerate 2 to 3 hours or overnight.

3. Preheat oven to 375°F.

4. Remove dough from the refrigerator. Slice cylinders into ¼-inch slices. Place on a parchment-lined cookie sheet, spacing each 2 inches apart.

5. Bake 10 to 12 minutes or until edges begin to brown. Remove cookie sheet from the oven. Using a metal spatula, remove cookies from the cookie sheet and place on a wire cooling rack. Cool completely. Store cookies refrigerated, in an airtight container.

YIELD: 60 COOKIES

CHAPTER 3

BAKERY FAVORITES

This section includes many bakery staples, popular not just at Sweet Maria's but at traditional bakeries across the country—good old-fashioned favorites like sugar cookies, hermits, and cheesecake squares. This is the type of cookie I made when I started at my first bakery job.

I've also included some cookies that are a part of our popular culture—cookies like pecan sandies, vanilla sandwiches, and newtons, cookies that we love but Mom *didn't* make. Whether they are made by elves, machine, Mom, or our neighborhood bakery, they are a delicious part of our lives. Plus, they're easy enough for you to bake at home.

VANILLA SUGAR COOKIES

These simply delicious cookies are great plain, or used as the basis for two
great variations: Stained Glass Cookies, and Black and White Cookies.
If you don't want to use a vanilla bean, you can use 1 teaspoon of
vanilla extract to flavor the cookie. Create your own shapes, sizes,
and designs by using any shape or size cookie cutter.

½ CUP SUGAR	2 CUPS FLOUR
1 VANILLA BEAN	2 TEASPOONS BAKING POWDER
1¼ STICKS BUTTER, SOFTENED	½ TEASPOON SALT
2 EGGS	ADDITIONAL SUGAR FOR DUSTING

1. Place sugar in a small mixing bowl. With a small paring knife, slice the vanilla bean lengthwise. Using the tip of the knife, scrape the vanilla seeds into the sugar. Mix until sugar and vanilla are well blended. Set aside.

2. In an electric mixer, cream the butter and vanilla sugar until light. Add eggs. Mix until well blended. On low speed, add flour, baking powder, and salt. Mix just until blended.

3. Wrap dough in plastic wrap and refrigerate 2 to 3 hours, or overnight.

4. Preheat oven to 350°F.

5. Roll dough out onto a lightly floured surface to ¼-inch thickness. Using a 2½-inch cookie cutter, cut dough into rounds. Place on a parchment-lined cookie sheet, spacing each 2 inches apart. Sprinkle tops with additional sugar.

6. Bake 10 to 12 minutes or until edges are lightly browned.

7. Remove cookie sheet from the oven. Using a metal spatula, remove cookies from the sheet and place on a wire cooling rack. Cool completely. Store in an airtight container.

YIELD: 30 2½-INCH COOKIES

STAINED GLASS WINDOWS

These cookies are our basic sugar cookie gone Hollywood.
Simply use a tiny cutter to cut out shapes from inside the cookie.
Fill these shapes with crushed hard candies in various colors. As they bake,
they become translucent. They're a fun project for holiday baking with
the kids. Be sure to roll these a bit thinner than sugar cookies.

1 RECIPE VANILLA SUGAR COOKIE
DOUGH (SEE PAGE 70)

ABOUT 4 OUNCES ASSORTED HARD
CANDIES

VARIOUS COOKIE CUTTERS IN
DIFFERENT SHAPES AND SIZES

1. Prepare vanilla sugar cookie dough. Refrigerate overnight.

2. Preheat oven to 375°F.

3. In a food processor, pulse hard candy into small crystals (like coarse salt). Chop each color separately. Set aside.

4. On a lightly floured surface, roll dough out to ⅛ inch thick. Using a 3-inch cutter, cut dough into rounds. Place on a parchment-lined cookie sheet. Using smaller cutters in various patterns, cut shapes out of dough circles. Re-roll and cut scraps of dough until all dough is used.

5. Using a small spoon, fill cut-out shapes with crushed candy.

6. Bake 10 to 12 minutes or until edges are lightly browned.

7. Remove cookie sheet from the oven. Cool cookies completely on parchment sheet. Store in an airtight container.

YIELD: 36 3-INCH COOKIES

BLACK AND WHITE COOKIES

This bakery classic is a basic sugar cookie that is frosted half with vanilla icing and half with chocolate icing. Popular since the nineteen forties, it was recently immortalized in a Seinfeld episode that focused on race relations and how we could all get along. "Look to the cookie. . . ." This version uses a tasty icing and a rich chocolate ganache to coat the cookies.

1 RECIPE VANILLA SUGAR COOKIE
(SEE PAGE 70)

1 RECIPE CHOCOLATE GANACHE
TOPPING (SEE PAGE 118) MADE
WITHOUT BUTTER

½ RECIPE COOKIE DECORATING
FROSTING (SEE PAGE 128)

1. Prepare dough and bake as described on page 70 for basic vanilla sugar cookies. Cut dough into 2½-inch circles. Bake and cool.

2. Using a small spatula or butter knife, spread chocolate ganache onto half of the cookie. Refrigerate until set. Frost other half of cookie with cookie decorating icing. Let cookies dry at room temperature. Store in an airtight container.

YIELD: 30 2½-INCH COOKIES

BUTTER COOKIES

*These classic buttery cookies are a specialty in many bakeries, including
Sweet Maria's. You can dress them up with a cherry or
walnut half before baking, or dip them in melted
chocolate after they're baked.*

½ POUND BUTTER, SOFTENED	½ TEASPOON BAKING POWDER
¾ CUP SUGAR	PINCH OF SALT
1 EGG	GLACÉ CHERRY HALVES, OPTIONAL
1 TEASPOON VANILLA EXTRACT	
2½ CUPS FLOUR	

1. Preheat oven to 350°F.

2. In an electric mixer, cream the butter and sugar until really fluffy, 3 to 4
   minutes. Add egg and vanilla. Mix until well blended.

3. On low speed, add flour, baking powder, and salt. Mix just until blended.
   Overmixing the dough will make it tough to squeeze from a pastry bag.

4. Fill a pastry bag with a large open star tip with the cookie dough. Pipe cookies
   onto a parchment-lined cookie sheet, spacing them 2 inches apart. If desired,
   place a cherry half in the center of each cookie before baking.

5. Bake 10 to 15 minutes, or until edges begin to brown.

6. Remove cookie sheet from the oven. Using a metal spatula, lift cookies off the
   cookie sheet and onto wire cooling racks. Cool completely. Store cookies in an
   airtight container.

YIELD: 40 COOKIES

Variation: Chocolate Butter Cookies

Add ½ cup cocoa when adding flour. Reduce flour to 2 cups.

IF YOU DON'T WANT TO USE A PASTRY BAG TO FORM COOKIES, YOU CAN USE THE FOLLOWING METHOD:

1. BREAK OFF A PIECE OF DOUGH AND ROLL IT INTO A 1-INCH BALL. IF THE DOUGH IS STICKY, LIGHTLY DUST YOUR FINGERS WITH FLOUR.
2. PLACE BALLS ON A PARCHMENT-LINED COOKIE SHEET, SPACING THEM 2 INCHES APART. PRESS THE TOPS OF THE BALLS TO FLATTEN.
3. DECORATE THE TOPS OF THE COOKIES USING A FORK IN A CRISS-CROSS FASHION. OR PLACE A NUT HALF OR CHERRY IN THE CENTER AND BAKE AS DIRECTED.

LEMON COCONUT MACAROONS

This lemon variation of the classic coconut macaroon has just the right amount of zip. Because they're a bit gooey, be sure to cool the cookies completely on parchment paper before removing.

3 CUPS COCONUT

²/₃ CUP SWEETENED CONDENSED MILK

GRATED RIND OF 1 LEMON

GRATED JUICE OF 1 LEMON

2 EGG WHITES

1. Preheat oven to 350°F.

2. In a medium bowl combine coconut, condensed milk, rind, and juice of one lemon. With a wooden spoon, mix until blended.

3. In an electric mixer, beat egg whites until stiff. Fold into coconut mixture. Drop dough from a teaspoon onto a parchment-lined cookie sheet, spacing each 2 inches apart.

4. Bake 10 to 12 minutes or until lightly browned.

5. Remove cookie sheet from the oven. Place cookie sheet on a wire cooling rack. Cool cookies completely on parchment. Do not remove until completely cool. Store in an airtight container.

YIELD: 36 COOKIES

RASPBERRY PINWHEELS

These refrigerator cookies have a spiral swirl of raspberry.
Rolling out the dough between 2 sheets of plastic wrap makes it
much easier to create the spiral effect. After making the "jelly roll" log,
just chill, slice, and bake. This is also the perfect cookie to make ahead.
Simply freeze cylinders of dough, and take them out of the freezer
and slice and bake whenever you want fresh cookies.

½ POUND BUTTER, SOFTENED	1 TEASPOON BAKING POWDER
1 CUP SUGAR	¼ TEASPOON SALT
2 EGG YOLKS	¼ CUP RASPBERRY JELLY
2½ CUPS FLOUR	

1. In an electric mixer, cream butter and sugar until light. Add egg yolks. Mix until well blended. On low speed, add 2¼ cups of the flour, baking powder, and salt. Mix just until blended. Dough should be stiff, not sticky.

2. Divide dough in half. Return half of dough to the mixer. On low speed, add raspberry jelly and remaining ¼ cup of flour. Mix until uniform in color.

3. Between 2 sheets of plastic, roll raspberry dough into a rectangle about 16 × 5 inches and ¼ inch thick. Remove plastic from top of dough.

4. Roll white dough the same way, to the same size, and remove plastic from top of dough. Using a pastry brush, wet the top of the raspberry dough with water. Carefully lay the white dough on top of the raspberry dough. Remove the plastic wrap from the top of the white dough. Using the plastic wrap underneath as a guide, roll the cookies lengthwise, jellyroll fashion. Cover the entire roll with plastic wrap and place seam side down on a cookie sheet. Refrigerate until firm, 2 to 3 hours or overnight.

5. Preheat oven to 375°F.

6. Remove cookie roll from the refrigerator. Using a sharp, straight knife, slice cookies into ¼-inch-thick slices. Place slices on a parchment-lined cookie sheet, spacing each 2 inches apart.

7. Bake 12 to 15 minutes or until edges begin to brown.

8. Remove cookie sheet from the oven. Using a metal spatula, remove cookies from the cookie sheet and place on a wire cooling rack. Cool completely.

YIELD: 40 COOKIES

◆ HOW TO ROLL BETWEEN SHEETS OF PLASTIC WRAP ◆

COOKIES LIKE RASPBERRY PINWHEELS AND FIG SWIRLS ARE EASY TO MANEUVER IF YOU ROLL THE DOUGH BETWEEN 2 SHEETS OF PLASTIC WRAP. PLACE DOUGH BETWEEN 2 SHEETS OF WRAP AND ROLL WITH A ROLLING PIN FROM THE CENTER OUT TO THE EDGES. FILL AND ASSEMBLE AS RECIPE DIRECTS. USING THE BOTTOM PIECE OF WRAP AS A GUIDE, ROLL DOUGH UP TIGHTLY, JELLYROLL FASHION.

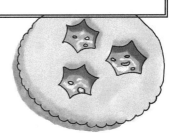

CHOCOLATE ESPRESSO CHECKERBOARDS

This version of another bakery classic combines two of my favorite flavors, coffee and chocolate. The dough is just about the same as the raspberry pinwheels, but these cookies have a flavor and style all their own.

1/2 POUND BUTTER, SOFTENED

1 CUP SUGAR

2 EGG YOLKS

2 1/4 CUPS FLOUR

1 TEASPOON BAKING POWDER

1/4 TEASPOON SALT

1/2 CUP CHOCOLATE CHIPS, MELTED

3 TEASPOONS INSTANT ESPRESSO POWDER

1. In an electric mixer, cream butter and sugar until light. Add egg yolks. Mix until well blended. On low speed, add flour, baking powder, and salt. Mix just until blended. Divide dough into 2 pieces, one slightly bigger than the other. In the smaller piece, mix in melted chocolate and instant espresso until well blended.

2. Divide white dough into 5 equal pieces. Roll each piece into a cylinder about 10 inches long. Flatten top and sides to form a square-sided rope, about 1/2 inch thick.

3. Divide chocolate dough into 4 equal pieces. Roll and shape these pieces the same as the white dough.

4. Stack the dough rectangles onto a piece of parchment paper. Arrange them white, chocolate, white, next to each other. Place remaining rectangles on top of these, alternating colors and stacking 3 rectangles high. Moisten each piece with water to adhere. Wrap entire cube of dough in plastic wrap and refrigerate until firm, 2 to 3 hours or overnight.

5. Preheat oven to 375°F.

6. Remove dough from the refrigerator. Using a sharp, straight knife, cut the dough into ¼-inch-thick slices. Place slices on a parchment-lined cookie sheet, spacing each 2 inches apart.

7. Bake 12 to 15 minutes, or until edges just begin to brown.

8. Remove cookie sheet from the oven. Using a metal spatula, remove cookies from the cookie sheet and place them on a wire cooling rack. Cool completely. Store cookies in an airtight container.

YIELD: 24 COOKIES

RUM BALLS

These no-bake cookies are based on an old bakery favorite that used stale cake crumbs instead of graham cracker crumbs. You can use any type of rum or any liqueur as long as it is high quality. These cookies are potent—so adults only, please!

2½ CUPS GRAHAM CRACKER CRUMBS

1 CUP CONFECTIONERS' SUGAR

½ CUP COCOA

½ CUP GLACÉ CHERRIES

½ CUP RAISINS

½ CUP WALNUTS, FINELY CHOPPED

½ CUP DARK RUM

¼ CUP CORN SYRUP

ADDITIONAL CONFECTIONERS' SUGAR FOR COATING COOKIES

1. In a large mixing bowl, combine graham cracker crumbs, confectioners' sugar, cocoa, glacé cherries, raisins, and walnuts. Mix with a wooden spoon. Add rum and corn syrup. Mix until well blended.

2. Roll dough into 1-inch balls. Dough may be sticky to roll. Dip hands in water for easier rolling. Roll balls in confectioners' sugar.

3. Place on parchment-lined cookie sheet or plate. Refrigerate until serving.

4. Store in an airtight container in the refrigerator. Serve chilled.

YIELD: 45

SOUR CREAM CUTOUTS

We bake these cookies for just about every holiday: trees and bells for Christmas, hearts for Valentine's Day, and flags for Flag Day. The sour cream and lemon combine for a great flavor and moisture. You can use butter instead of margarine, but it will be harder to roll out, especially when chilled.

1 1/2 STICKS MARGARINE, SOFTENED	1/2 TEASPOON LEMON EXTRACT
3/4 CUP SUGAR	1/4 CUP SOUR CREAM
1 EGG	3 CUPS FLOUR
1/2 TEASPOON VANILLA EXTRACT	2 TEASPOONS BAKING POWDER

1. In an electric mixer, on medium speed, cream margarine and sugar until light. Add egg, vanilla, and lemon extract. Mix until well blended. Add sour cream. Mix well.

2. On low speed, add flour and baking powder. Mix just until blended.

3. Wrap dough in plastic wrap and refrigerate overnight.

4. Preheat oven to 350°F.

5. Divide dough in half. Keep other half in refrigerator. Roll dough to 1/4 inch thick. Cut into desired shapes. Repeat with other half of the dough. Save scraps for the end and re-roll until all dough is used.

6. Place cookies onto a parchment-lined cookie sheet, spacing each 2 inches apart.

7. Bake 10 to 12 minutes or until firm and edges are just browned.

8. Remove cookie sheet from the oven. Using a metal spatula, remove cookies from the sheet and place on a wire cooling rack. Cool completely.

9. Frost and decorate as desired.

YIELD: 30 3-INCH DAISY COOKIES

HOW TO DECORATE SOUR CREAM CUTOUTS

There are several ways to decorate sour cream cutouts, depending on what type of look you'd like, and how much time you can spend decorating. The sky is the limit for your own creativity for decorating these cookies. Here are a couple of methods:

WATER WASH AND COLORED SUGARS

The simplest way to decorate cutout cookies is to brush the tops with water, and sprinkle with colored sugars. This should be done before baking.

You can also add food coloring right to the dough for an extra burst of color. You can also marble the dough by adding food color and not blending the color totally together. This will give the cookies an interesting design and texture.

FROSTED COOKIES

To frost these cutouts we use cookie decorating frosting (see page 128). To get a smooth finish on cookies, add a bit of water to the icing so it spreads smoothly. Let cookies dry completely before piping on designs or monograms, especially if you are using another color. The colors may bleed if the base color is not completely dry.

HAND-PAINTED COOKIES

This method of decorating gives the cookies a hand-painted watercolor style. After baking, frost cookies with cookie decorating frosting (see page 128). Let cookies dry completely. Using a clean paint brush and food coloring, paint desired designs. I prefer to use paste food coloring. I will take a bit of color from the jar and place it on a small piece of aluminum foil. This will be my palette. Dip your paintbrush in water to get a lighter shade of the color you are using. You can also mix colors on this aluminum foil palette. We use this technique for springtime cookies. Frost a 4-inch round cookie with white icing. Let dry. Paint on bright yellow or red tulips with stems and leaves. For summer, we paint bright sunflowers or daisies.

PIPING FROSTING ONTO COOKIES

You can decorate cutout cookies with a pastry bag, too. We use this technique for daisies, sunflowers, and poinsettia cookies. All these flowers use the same petal flower cookie cutter, about 3 inches in diameter. The frosting will need to be a little stiffer to hold the design you're piping. Bake cookies shaped with a daisy-type petal flower cutter. Pipe petals from the center to the edge with tip #32 for daisies, tip #67 for sunflowers, and tip #352 for poinsettias. With tip #32 for daisies, pipe a different color center into the middle of the cookie (brown for sunflower center). Use tip #3 in yellow for poinsettias. Let cookies dry completely.

You can also frost cookies, then pipe on monograms, or pipe on sports logos or college logos. These personal types of cookies make ideal favors for weddings or showers. I've done dresses and wedding cake cookies for these occasions, as well as tropical fish, ladybugs, and farm animals.

LEMON POPPY BARS

These bars have a zesty lemon topping and a tender, buttery crust. You can either grease the baking pan or line it with aluminum foil for easy removal.

CRUST:

¼ POUND BUTTER, SOFTENED

½ CUP CONFECTIONERS' SUGAR

1 CUP FLOUR

1 TABLESPOON POPPY SEEDS

FILLING:

2 EGGS

1 CUP SUGAR

JUICE OF 1 LEMON

GRATED RIND OF 1 LEMON

½ TEASPOON BAKING POWDER

1 TABLESPOON FLOUR

CONFECTIONERS' SUGAR FOR DUSTING

1. Preheat oven to 350°F.

2. In an electric mixer, cream butter and confectioners' sugar until light. On low speed, add flour and poppy seeds. Mix just until blended.

3. Press crust into a greased 8 × 8 × 2-inch baking pan.

4. Bake 8 to 10 minutes or until edges begin to brown. Remove pan from the oven.

5. With a wire whisk, mix eggs and sugar until light. Add lemon juice, lemon rind, baking powder, and flour. Mix until smooth.

6. Pour filling over crust. Bake 10 to 12 minutes or until lightly browned and the center is set.

7. Remove pan from the oven. Cool completely in pan on wire cooling rack. Dust with confectioners' sugar. Cover pan with plastic wrap and refrigerate. Cut into squares as needed.

8. Store unused bars in the refrigerator.

YIELD: 20 SQUARES.

CLASSIC GINGERSNAPS

Gingersnaps are always in season. This recipe is the best I've ever tried, a family secret shared by my friend Betsy. Be sure to bake the cookies until evenly browned to get that gingersnap "snap." If they're undercooked, they'll still be tasty but chewy. Be sure to space them 3 inches apart because they will spread during baking.

²/₃ CUP VEGETABLE OIL	1 TEASPOON GINGER
1 CUP SUGAR	1 TEASPOON SALT
1 EGG	2 TEASPOONS BAKING SODA
⅓ CUP MOLASSES	1 TEASPOON CREAM OF TARTAR
1½ TO 1¾ CUPS FLOUR	ADDITIONAL SUGAR FOR COATING COOKIES
1 TEASPOON CINNAMON	

1. Preheat oven to 350°F.

2. In an electric mixer on medium speed, beat oil and sugar. Add egg and molasses. Beat until well mixed.

3. On low speed, add flour, cinnamon, ginger, salt, baking soda, and cream of tartar. Mix just until blended.

4. Roll dough into 1-inch balls. Roll in additional sugar. Place onto a parchment-lined cookie sheet, spacing each 3 inches apart.

5. Bake 12 to 15 minutes or until well browned.

6. Remove cookie sheet from oven. Using a metal spatula, remove cookies from sheet and place on a wire cooling rack. Cool completely. Store cookies in an airtight container.

YIELD: ABOUT 30 COOKIES

PECAN SANDIES

These cookies have a truly nostalgic bakery taste. The sugar gives them their sandy texture, with just the right amount of crunch. They're easy to bake and can be made with any nut you like.

1 CUP SHORTENING	1 ½ CUPS FLOUR
1 CUP SUGAR	1 TEASPOON SALT
1 TEASPOON VANILLA EXTRACT	1 TEASPOON BAKING SODA
1 EGG	1 CUP PECANS, CHOPPED

1. In an electric mixer, cream shortening and sugar. Add vanilla and egg. Mix until well blended.

2. On low speed, add flour, salt, and baking soda. Stir in nuts.

3. Divide dough into 3 equal pieces. On a lightly floured surface, roll dough into cylinders about 12 to 14 inches long. Wrap in plastic wrap and refrigerate 2 to 3 hours or overnight.

4. Preheat oven to 350°F.

5. Remove dough from the refrigerator. Cut into ¼-inch-thick slices and place on a parchment-lined cookie sheet, spacing each 2 inches apart.

6. Bake 10 to 12 minutes or until golden brown.

7. Remove cookie sheet from the oven. Using a metal spatula, remove cookies from the cookie sheet and place on a wire cooling rack. Cool completely.

8. Store cookies in an airtight container at room temperature.

YIELD: 50 COOKIES

FIG SWIRLS

These fig-filled cookies are always a favorite.
The technique is similar to the one used for Raspberry Pinwheels.
Rolling the dough between two sheets of plastic wrap really
helps to maneuver the dough into a log.

CRUST:

1/4 POUND BUTTER, SOFTENED

1 CUP SUGAR

1 EGG

1 1/2 CUPS FLOUR

1/2 TEASPOON SALT

1/2 TEASPOON BAKING SODA

FILLING:

1/2 POUND DRIED FIGS

1/4 CUP SUGAR

1/4 CUP WATER

1/2 CUP WALNUTS, CHOPPED

1. Prepare crust. In an electric mixer, cream butter and sugar until light. Add egg. Mix until well blended. On low speed, gradually add flour, salt, and baking soda. Mix just until blended. Divide dough in half. Wrap in plastic wrap and refrigerate overnight.

2. Prepare filling. Combine all ingredients in a food processor. Pulse for 15 to 20 seconds or just until blended. Set aside.

3. Between two sheets of plastic wrap, roll out half the dough into a rectangle about 16 × 4 inches. Spread half the filling over the dough, leaving about 1/4 inch all along the edges. Roll lengthwise, jellyroll fashion, using the plastic to help you roll. Place on a parchment-lined cookie sheet. Repeat with other half of dough and filling. Cover completely with plastic wrap and refrigerate 3 to 4 hours or overnight.

4. Preheat oven to 350°F. Remove plastic wrap. Slice dough into 1/4-inch slices and place cut side up onto a parchment-lined cookie sheet.

5. Bake 10 to 12 minutes or until lightly browned.

6. Remove cookie sheet from the oven. Using a metal spatula, remove cookies from the cookie sheet and place on a wire cooling rack. Cool completely. Store cookies in an airtight container at room temperature.

YIELD: 50 COOKIES

◆ **COOKIE JARS** ◆

WHEN I WAS GROWING UP, WE HAD QUITE A VARIETY OF COOKIE JARS, FROM PLAIN CANISTERS TO A LARGE GREEN PEAR. MY FAVORITE WAS A BRIGHT YELLOW SMILEY FACE, THE ULTIMATE SYMBOL OF HAPPINESS FROM THE 1970S. MANY PEOPLE COLLECT COOKIE JARS, AND SOME ARE NOW WORTH A LOT OF MONEY. MY APPROACH TO COOKIE JAR COLLECTING IS TO LET PERSONAL TASTE AND STYLE BE MY GUIDE.

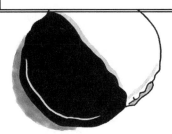

VANILLA SANDWICHES

*These classic sandwich cookies are like a homemade vanilla Oreo.
They are a nostalgic treat that can very easily be made at
home. For a lemon filling variation, add the grated
rind and juice of one lemon to the filling.*

DOUGH:

1/2 CUP SHORTENING

1/4 POUND BUTTER, SOFTENED

1 CUP SUGAR

1 EGG YOLK

1 TEASPOON VANILLA EXTRACT

1 3/4 CUPS FLOUR

PINCH OF SALT

FILLING:

4 CUPS CONFECTIONERS' SUGAR

6 TABLESPOONS BUTTER, MELTED AND COOLED

2 TEASPOONS VANILLA EXTRACT

6 TABLESPOONS HEAVY CREAM

1. Prepare dough. In an electric mixer, on medium speed, cream shortening and butter until well blended. Add sugar and mix until light. Add egg yolk and vanilla. Mix until blended.

2. On low speed, add flour and salt. Mix just until blended. Divide dough into two equal pieces. Wrap in plastic wrap. Refrigerate overnight.

3. Preheat oven to 350°F. Remove dough from the refrigerator. Roll dough out onto a lightly floured surface. Roll very thin, about 1/8 inch thick. Using a 2-inch round cookie cutter, cut dough into rounds. Place on a parchment-lined cookie sheet, spacing each 2 inches apart. Using a fork, prick holes in the center of the cookies. Repeat rolling and cutting remaining dough, re-rolling all the scraps at the end.

4. Bake 10 to 12 minutes or until edges just begin to brown.

5. Remove cookie sheet from the oven. Using a metal spatula, remove cookies from the cookie sheet and place on a wire cooling rack. Cool completely.

6. Prepare filling. In an electric mixer, combine confectioners' sugar, butter, vanilla, and heavy cream. Mix until well blended and smooth.

7. Assemble sandwiches. Pair off cookies to matching pairs. Using a butter knife or small spatula, spread a generous amount of frosting on the underside of one cookie. Press another matching cookie firmly together to form sandwich.

8. Continue to fill all cookies. Let dry. Store unused cookies at room temperature in an airtight container.

YIELD: 40 COOKIES

HONEY CINNAMON COOKIES

*These are hearty sugar cookies topped with cinnamon and sugar.
The honey in the dough really adds another depth of
flavor to this seemingly simple cookie.*

¾ CUP SHORTENING	TOPPING:
½ CUP SUGAR	3 TABLESPOONS SUGAR
1 EGG	2 TEASPOONS CINNAMON
½ CUP HONEY	½ CUP WALNUTS, FINELY CHOPPED
2¼ CUPS FLOUR	

1. In an electric mixer, cream shortening and sugar until light. Add egg and honey. Mix until well blended. On low speed, add flour. Mix just until blended. Wrap dough in plastic wrap and refrigerate overnight.

2. Preheat oven to 350°F.

3. In a small bowl, combine sugar, cinnamon, and walnuts. Set aside.

4. Using a rolling pin, roll dough out onto a lightly floured surface, about ¼ inch thick. Using a 3-inch round cookie cutter, cut dough into circles. Place on a parchment-lined cookie sheet, spacing each 2 inches apart. Brush the tops of the cookie with water. Sprinkle generously with topping.

5. Bake 10 to 12 minutes or until edges begin to brown.

6. Remove cookie sheet from the oven. Using a metal spatula, remove cookies from the cookie sheet and place on a wire cooling rack. Cool. Store cookies in an airtight container at room temperature.

YIELD: 20 COOKIES

STRAWBERRY JELL-O LOLLIPOP COOKIES

These cookies are like fruity shortbreads on a stick, and perfect fun for kids to make and take for a lunchtime treat. You can use any flavor Jell-O—that'll give you a variety of options for flavor and color.

¾ CUP BUTTER, SOFTENED	2 CUPS FLOUR
½ CUP SUGAR	¼ TEASPOON SALT
2 EGGS	40 4-INCH LOLLIPOP STICKS
1 PACKAGE STRAWBERRY JELL-O	COARSE SANDING SUGAR
1 TEASPOON BAKING POWDER	

1. Preheat oven to 350°F.

2. In an electric mixer, cream the butter and the sugar until light. Add eggs. Mix until well blended.

3. On low speed, add Jell-O, flour, baking powder, and salt. Mix just until well blended. Roll dough into 1-inch balls. Place on a parchment-lined cookie sheet, spacing each 2 inches apart and leaving enough space between rows for half the length of the lollipop sticks. Use a cookie stamp or bottom of a juice glass to press cookies flat, to ¼ inch thick.

4. Dip end of lollipop stick in water and insert halfway into the cookie. Lightly brush cookies with water and sprinkle on sanding sugar.

5. Bake 10 to 12 minutes or until edges begin to brown.

6. Remove cookie sheet from the oven. Using a metal spatula, remove cookies from the cookie sheet and place on a wire cooling rack. Cool completely. Wrap top cookie portion only in cellophane or colored plastic wrap. Tie tightly around the neck with a colorful ribbon.

YIELD: 40 COOKIE LOLLIPOPS

BANANA DATE NUT NEWTONS

These filled cookie rolls have a rich combination of flavors.
They're a perfect treat for any occasion and
look fantastic on cookie trays.

CRUST:

¼ POUND BUTTER, SOFTENED

1 CUP SUGAR

2 EGGS

2½ CUPS FLOUR

¼ TEASPOON BAKING SODA

PINCH OF SALT

FILLING:

2 RIPE BANANAS

½ CUP SUGAR

8 OUNCES DATES, CHOPPED

½ CUP FLOUR

1 CUP WALNUTS

1. Prepare crust. In an electric mixer, on medium speed, cream butter and sugar until light. Add eggs. Mix until well blended. On low speed, add 2 cups flour, baking soda, and salt. Mix just until blended.

2. Turn dough out onto a lightly floured surface. Knead in remaining ½ cup of flour to make dough soft, but not sticky. Divide dough in half. Wrap in plastic wrap and refrigerate 4 to 5 hours or overnight.

3. Preheat oven to 350°F.

4. In a food processor, combine all filling ingredients. Pulse until almost smooth. Refrigerate filling while rolling out the crust.

5. Roll half of the dough out onto a lightly floured surface. Roll into a rectangle measuring approximately 16 × 8 inches. Cut dough into two strips measuring 16 × 4 inches. Working with one strip at a time, spoon one-quarter of the filling down the middle of the dough lengthwise. Fold both sides over to seal.

6. Place on a parchment-lined cookie sheet, seam side down. Refrigerate 20 to 30 minutes. Remove filled cookies from the refrigerator. Cut into ¼-inch strips.

7. Place on a parchment-lined cookie sheet, spacing each 2 inches apart. Be sure to place the seam side down. Repeat with other half of dough.

8. Bake 12 to 15 minutes or until lightly browned.

9. Remove cookie sheet from the oven. Using a metal spatula, remove cookies from the cookie sheet and place on a wire cooling rack. Cool completely.

YIELD: 36–40 COOKIES

◆ COOKIE NAMES ◆

I LOVE COOKIE NAMES. SO MANY OF THEM REFLECT WHAT THE COOKIE IS ALL ABOUT. THE NAMES CHEWIES, CRUNCHIES, BROWNIES, AND SANDIES REALLY DESCRIBE THE COOKIES' TEXTURES. OTHER NAMES SUCH AS DROPS, SQUARES, AND CUTOUTS ARE NAMED FOR THE TECHNIQUES USED TO MAKE THEM. COOKIE NAMES SUCH AS SNICKERDOODLES AND NEWTONS ARE STILL QUITE MYSTERIOUS.

HERMITS

*These hearty cookies were a specialty of the first bakery I
worked in, Rita's, and this recipe uses the same style, resulting in
Hermits that have a great combination of spice, nuts, and raisins.
The dough is flattened on the cookie sheet in strips,
baked, and then cut into 3-inch cookies.*

*Hermits are a New England specialty. The name refers
to leaving these cookies alone to let their spices
blend and age before eating.*

1/4 POUND BUTTER, SOFTENED	1 1/2 TEASPOONS BAKING SODA
1 CUP SUGAR	1/2 TEASPOON SALT
1 EGG	1 1/2 CUPS RAISINS
1/3 CUP MOLASSES	1/2 CUP WALNUTS, FINELY CHOPPED
1/2 CUP MILK	
3 CUPS FLOUR	1 EGG FOR EGG WASH
2 TEASPOONS CINNAMON	ADDITIONAL SUGAR FOR DUSTING
1 1/2 TEASPOONS GINGER	

1. In an electric mixer, cream butter and sugar until light. Add egg, molasses, and milk. Mix until well blended.

2. On low speed, add flour, cinnamon, ginger, baking soda, and salt. Mix just until blended. Stir in raisins and walnuts.

3. Divide dough into quarters. Wrap in plastic wrap and refrigerate dough 2 to 3 hours or overnight.

4. Preheat oven to 350°F.

5. Roll each piece of dough into a cylinder the length of a cookie sheet. Press dough into a strip 3 inches wide and ¼ inch thick on a parchment-lined cookie sheet. Space each strip 2 inches apart.

6. In a small bowl, beat egg. Using a pastry brush, brush each strip with egg and sprinkle with additional sugar.

7. Bake 15 to 20 minutes or until dark brown.

8. Remove cookie sheet from the oven. While cookies are still hot, cut into 3-inch pieces. Cool cookies on parchment. Cool completely.

9. Store cookies in an airtight container at room temperature.

YIELD: 24 COOKIES

CAPPUCCINO DROPS

These cookies deliver a great combination of coffee and cinnamon. They're easy to make and are a perfect companion to a cup of hot coffee and a good book.

½ **POUND BUTTER, SOFTENED**	2¼ **CUPS FLOUR**
1¼ **CUPS SUGAR**	1 **TEASPOON CINNAMON**
3 **TEASPOONS INSTANT ESPRESSO POWDER**	1 **TEASPOON BAKING SODA**
	½ **TEASPOON SALT**
2 **EGGS**	
1 **TABLESPOON COFFEE LIQUEUR**	

1. Preheat oven to 350°F.

2. In an electric mixer, cream butter and sugar until light. Add espresso powder, eggs, and coffee liqueur. Mix until well blended.

3. On low speed, add flour, cinnamon, baking soda, and salt. Mix just until well blended.

4. Drop dough from a teaspoon onto a parchment-lined cookie sheet, spacing each 2 inches apart.

5. Bake 10 to 12 minutes or until lightly browned.

6. Remove cookie sheet from the oven. Using a metal spatula, remove cookies and place on a wire cooling rack. Cool completely. Store cookies at room temperature in an airtight container.

YIELD: 50 COOKIES

PRUNE BARS

*These delicious bars were a specialty of the first bakery
I worked in. They have a crumblike crust and
topping and a rich, flavorful center.*

CRUST:

1½ CUPS FLOUR

1½ CUPS OATS

1 CUP BROWN SUGAR

1 TEASPOON BAKING SODA

1½ STICKS BUTTER, SOFTENED

FILLING:

12 OUNCES DRIED PRUNES

¼ CUP SUGAR

1 CUP WALNUTS, COARSELY CHOPPED

1. Preheat oven to 350°F.

2. Grease and flour or spray with nonstick baking spray a 13 × 9-inch baking pan. Set aside.

3. Prepare crust. In a medium bowl, combine flour, oats, brown sugar, and baking soda. Mix well. Add butter and cut in with a pastry cutter until mixture resembles coarse crumbs.

4. Press three-quarters of the mixture into the prepared pan. Set aside the rest of the crumb mixture.

5. Prepare filling. In a food processor, pulse prunes and sugar until coarse. Sprinkle mixture over the top of crust. Sprinkle walnuts over prune mixture. Top with remaining crumb mixture. Press the top gently.

6. Bake 25 to 30 minutes or until golden brown.

7. Remove pan from the oven. Place on a wire cooling rack. Cool in pan completely. Cover pan with plastic wrap. Store bars in pan at room temperature. Cut into squares as needed.

YIELD: 24 SQUARES

MINT SHORTBREADS

These are a special summertime refresher, although you can make them all year round if you have a supply of fresh mint. They are perfect served with your favorite ice cream (mine is chocolate).

1 ½ STICKS BUTTER, SOFTENED

1 CUP CONFECTIONERS' SUGAR

1 ⅓ CUPS FLOUR

3 TABLESPOONS CORNSTARCH

PINCH OF SALT

3 TABLESPOONS FRESH MINT, FINELY CHOPPED

ADDITIONAL SUGAR FOR SPRINKLING TOPS

1. Preheat oven to 350°F.

2. In an electric mixer, cream butter and confectioners' sugar until light. On low speed, add flour, cornstarch, salt, and mint. Mix just until blended.

3. Roll dough out onto a lightly floured surface. Roll to about a 10-inch square, about ⅛ inch thick. Using a sharp, straight knife, cut dough into 2-inch squares. Cut squares diagonally into triangles. Irregular shapes are okay.

4. Place cookies onto a parchment-lined cookie sheet, spacing each 2 inches apart. Sprinkle tops with granulated sugar.

5. Bake 10 to 12 minutes or until edges begin to brown.

6. Remove cookie sheet from the oven. Using a metal spatula, remove cookies from the cookie sheet and place on a wire cooling rack. Cool completely. Store cookies at room temperature in an airtight container.

YIELD: 30 COOKIES

BRASS CITY BARS

These cookies are named for my hometown, Waterbury, Connecticut, which was once the brass capital of the world. Waterbury today has all kinds of chips and we're all a little nuts to live here. But these bars, like the citizens here, are sweet and friendly. You can use any combination of chips in this recipe— in fact, it's a delicious way to make use of a variety of leftover chips.

CRUST:

1 CUP FLOUR

¾ CUP OATS

½ CUP SUGAR

½ TEASPOON BAKING SODA

¼ TEASPOON SALT

¼ POUND BUTTER, SOFTENED

FILLING:

½ CUP CARAMEL ICE CREAM TOPPING

½ CUP WALNUTS, CHOPPED

½ CUP PEANUT BUTTER CHIPS

½ CUP WHITE CHOCOLATE CHIPS

½ CUP CHOCOLATE CHIPS

1. Preheat oven to 350°F.

2. Prepare crust. In a food processor, combine flour, oats, sugar, baking soda, and salt. Add butter and pulse just until mixture resembles coarse crumbs. Reserve and set aside 1 cup of crust.

3. Grease an 8 × 8 × 2-inch baking pan. Press crumb mixture evenly into the bottom of the pan. Bake 10 to 12 minutes or until lightly browned.

4. Pour caramel topping over the hot crust. Evenly sprinkle nuts, peanut butter chips, white chocolate chips, and chocolate chips over the caramel. Sprinkle with remaining crust. Gently press together.

5. Bake 15 to 20 minutes or until lightly browned.

6. Remove pan from the oven. Place pan on a wire cooling rack. Cool completely. Cut into squares. Store unused cookies in an airtight container.

YIELD: 20 SQUARES

CHEESECAKE SQUARES

These cheesecake bars can be flavored with a variety
of toppings. It's the perfect way to satisfy
a craving for cheesecake.

CRUST:

1 1/2 STICKS BUTTER, SOFTENED

1/2 CUP SUGAR

1 1/2 CUPS FLOUR

FILLING:

8 OUNCES CREAM CHEESE

1 CUP SUGAR

1/4 CUP FLOUR

4 EGGS

TOPPING:

1/2 CUP PINEAPPLE OR ANY FLAVOR
PRESERVE

1. Preheat oven to 350°F.

2. Prepare crust. In an electric mixer, cream butter and sugar until light. On low speed, add flour. Mix just until blended. Press dough into an ungreased 13 × 9-inch baking pan. Bake 12 to 15 minutes or until lightly browned. Remove from the oven.

3. Prepare filling. In an electric mixer, mix cream cheese and sugar until light and smooth. Add flour. Add eggs, one at a time, beating well after adding each one. Mix until smooth. Pour filling over hot crust.

4. Bake 20 to 25 minutes or until edges begin to brown and center is set.

5. Remove pan from the oven and place on a wire cooling rack. Cool completely.

6. Spread preserves evenly over filling. Refrigerate 2 to 3 hours or overnight. Cut into squares. Serve chilled. Store cookies in refrigerator.

YIELD: 24 SQUARES

ALMOND TRIANGLES

These bars are a star at Sweet Maria. The buttery crust is topped
with a sweet combination of almonds, sugar, and honey.
For easier cutting, refrigerate before slicing.

CRUST:

½ POUND BUTTER, SOFTENED

½ CUP SUGAR

1 EGG

2 CUPS FLOUR

TOPPING:

¼ POUND BUTTER

¼ CUP BROWN SUGAR

½ CUP HONEY

1½ CUPS SLICED ALMONDS

2 TABLESPOONS HEAVY CREAM

1. Preheat oven to 375°F.

2. Prepare crust. In an electric mixer, cream butter and sugar. Add egg. Mix well. On low speed, add flour and mix just until blended. Press dough into the bottom and slightly up the sides of a 14 × 10-inch greased jellyroll pan.

3. Bake 10 to 15 minutes or until lightly browned. Remove pan from the oven.

4. Prepare topping. In a medium saucepan on medium-high heat, combine butter, brown sugar, and honey. Stir often until butter melts, sugar dissolves, and mixture comes to a boil. Remove from the heat. Stir in almonds and heavy cream. Spread almond mixture on top of the crust.

5. Bake 10 to 12 minutes or until top begins to bubble and brown.

6. Remove pan from the oven. Place pan on a wire cooling rack. Cool cookies completely in pan. Refrigerate. Cut into squares. Cut squares in half, diagonally, to form triangles. Store cookies in refrigerator in an airtight container.

YIELD: 50 TRIANGLES

CHAPTER 4

CHOCOLATE COOKIES AND SIMPLE CANDIES

This chapter spotlights everyone's favorite flavor, chocolate. What flavor is better for comfort or indulgence than chocolate? Here you'll find some classics, like fudge brownies and toffee bars, as well as new creations, such as *Chocolat*-inspired chili pepper cookies and chocolate Nutella sandwiches. The cookie jar always empties quicker whenever chocolate cookies are the cookie of the day, and I hope you'll see why.

Most of the recipes in this collection use semisweet chocolate, milk chocolate, dark chocolate, or white chocolate. You can certainly substitute one for the other, depending on your personal preference. Chocolate is satisfying on its own or paired with great partners such as peanut butter, nuts, cherries, and orange.

A few of the recipes in this chapter are more like a candy than a cookie. Treats such as fudge and peanut butter balls are hard to classify. Whatever you call them, they are a delicious snack, and a perfect gift for that chocoholic in everyone.

FUDGE BROWNIES

Classic chocolate brownies are the ultimate treat with a glass of cold milk. These do not disappoint. Some people have trouble testing for the doneness of brownies. Using a cake tester or a toothpick, the center should have a slight crumb on it, not batter. Many consider this to be undercooked, but the brownie will continue to bake in the pan when removed from the oven.

1/4 POUND BUTTER, SOFTENED	3/4 CUP COCOA
2 CUPS SUGAR	1 CUP FLOUR
1 TEASPOON VANILLA EXTRACT	1/2 TEASPOON BAKING POWDER
4 EGGS	1/4 TEASPOON SALT

1. Preheat oven to 350°F.

2. Grease a 13 × 9-inch baking pan. Set aside.

3. In an electric mixer, cream butter and sugar until light. Add vanilla. Add eggs one at a time, beating well after adding each one. Mix until well blended. On low speed, add cocoa, flour, baking powder, and salt. Beat until well blended. Pour batter into prepared pan. Using a metal spatula, spread batter evenly.

4. Bake 25 to 30 minutes or until batter begins to pull away from the sides. Check the center with a toothpick or cake tester. There should be a slight crumb, but it should not be wet in the middle.

5. Remove pan from the oven. Place on a wire cooling rack. Cool completely in pan. Cover pan with plastic wrap and store at room temperature. Cut into squares as needed or cut into squares and wrap individually in plastic wrap.

YIELD: 24 BROWNIES

TOFFEE BARS

You can use any brand of toffee bars to make these delicious and sweet bar cookies. The Sweet Maria staff is usually the first to empty the cookie jar when these cookies are around!

CRUST:

4 TABLESPOONS BUTTER, SOFTENED

1/2 CUP BROWN SUGAR

1 CUP FLOUR

FILLING:

1/4 POUND BUTTER

1/4 CUP BROWN SUGAR

1 CUP CRUSHED TOFFEE BARS

1. Preheat oven to 350°F.

2. In an electric mixer on low speed, mix butter, brown sugar, and flour. Mix until mixture resembles coarse crumbs.

3. Press crust mixture into an 8 × 8 × 2-inch baking dish.

4. In a medium saucepan, combine butter and brown sugar. Bring to a boil, stirring constantly. Pour over crust. Sprinkle with crushed toffee bars.

5. Bake 15 to 20 minutes or until lightly browned.

6. Remove pan from the oven. Cool cookies completely in pan on a wire cooling rack. Cover pan with plastic wrap and store at room temperature. Cut into squares as needed or cut into squares and wrap individually in plastic wrap.

YIELD: 20 SQUARES

CHOCOLATE NUTELLA SANDWICHES

These are grown-up double-chocolate sandwich cookies with an Italian accent. The filling is a popular Italian chocolate and hazelnut spread called Nutella. You can find it at most supermarkets and specialty food stores. These cookies are very tender, so be sure they're completely cool before assembling.

½ POUND BUTTER, SOFTENED

¾ CUP SUGAR

1 ¼ CUPS FLOUR

½ CUP COCOA

FILLING:

1 CUP NUTELLA

1. Preheat oven to 350°F.

2. In an electric mixer, on medium speed, cream butter and sugar until light. On low speed, gradually add flour and cocoa. Mix just until well blended.

3. Roll dough into 1-inch balls. Place on a parchment-lined cookie sheet, spacing each 2 inches apart. If dough is sticky, dust your fingers with additional cocoa. Using a fork lightly dusted in cocoa, press tops of cookies to flatten.

4. Bake 12 to 15 minutes or until firm.

5. Remove cookie sheet from the oven. Using a metal spatula, remove cookies from the cookie sheet and place on a wire cooling rack. Cool completely.

6. To assemble, pair cookies of similar size tops and bottoms. Using a small metal spatula, spread some Nutella on the bottom of one cookie. Press another cookie, bottom first, to form a sandwich. Press together gently. Let dry on a wire cooling rack. Store at room temperatue.

YIELD: 14 2½-INCH COOKIES

CHOCOLATE CHIP PECAN BLONDIES

Do these cookies have more fun? These pecan-packed bars are a not-so-chocolate alternative to brownies. Try them topped with your favorite ice cream and a drizzle of fudge sauce.

1 ½ STICKS BUTTER, SOFTENED	1 ¾ CUPS FLOUR
1 ½ CUPS BROWN SUGAR	1 TEASPOON BAKING POWDER
½ CUP SUGAR	PINCH OF SALT
2 EGGS	1 CUP CHOCOLATE CHIPS
1 TEASPOON VANILLA EXTRACT	1 CUP PECANS, COARSELY CHOPPED

1. Preheat oven to 350°F.

2. Grease a 13 × 9-inch pan. Set aside.

3. In an electric mixer, cream butter, brown sugar, and sugar until light. Add eggs and vanilla. Mix well.

4. On low speed, add flour, baking powder, and salt. Mix just until blended. Stir in chocolate chips and pecans.

5. Spread into prepared pan.

6. Bake 25 to 30 minutes. Check center with a cake tester or toothpick. There should be a slight crumb, but it should not be wet in the middle.

7. Remove pan from the oven. Place on a wire cooling rack. Cool completely in pan. Cover pan with plastic wrap and store at room temperature. Cut into squares as needed or cut into squares and wrap individually in plastic wrap.

YIELD: 24 SQUARES

CHOCOLATE ORANGE BISCOTTI

*The complementary flavors of chocolate and orange combine
to give these biscotti a rich and satisfying taste. Enjoy
them with a cup of cappuccino or hot chocolate.*

¼ POUND BUTTER, SOFTENED	3 EGGS
¾ CUP SUGAR	2 CUPS FLOUR
2 TEASPOONS INSTANT ESPRESSO POWDER	½ CUP COCOA
GRATED RIND OF 1 ORANGE	3 TEASPOONS BAKING POWDER
JUICE OF 1 ORANGE	PINCH OF SALT

1. Preheat oven to 375° F.

2. In an electric mixer, cream butter, sugar, and instant espresso powder.

3. Add rind, juice, and eggs. Mix until well blended.

4. On low speed, add flour, cocoa, baking powder, and salt. Mix until just blended.

5. Turn dough out onto a lightly floured surface. Divide dough into 3 equal portions. Roll dough into a cylinder. Place on a parchment-lined cookie sheet, spacing each 3 inches apart.

6. Bake 20 to 25 minutes or until firm.

7. Remove cookie sheet from the oven. Using two metal spatulas, carefully remove loaves from the hot cookie sheet onto wire cooling racks. Cool. Place cooled loaves on a cutting board. Using a sharp knife, slice the loaves diagonally into ½-inch-wide slices.

8. Place the slices on a cookie sheet in a single layer. Return to the oven for 12 to 15 minutes, or until lightly browned. Remove cookie sheet from the oven. Cool toasted biscotti on a wire cooling rack. Store in an airtight container.

YIELD: 24 BISCOTTI

CHOCOLATE ALMOND HEARTS

*These sweet somethings are the perfect Valentine treat. Serve them
plain, or dipped or drizzled in chocolate. You can enjoy
them any time of the year, in any shape.*

½ POUND MARGARINE, SOFTENED	½ CUP COCOA
1 CUP CONFECTIONERS' SUGAR	1½ CUPS FLOUR
2 TEASPOONS ALMOND EXTRACT	¼ TEASPOON SALT

1. In an electric mixer on medium speed, cream the margarine and confectioners' sugar until light. Add almond extract.

2. On low speed, add cocoa, flour, and salt. Mix just until well blended. Wrap dough in plastic wrap and refrigerate 2 to 3 hours or overnight.

3. Preheat oven to 350°F.

4. Roll out dough about ¼-inch thick onto a surface lightly dusted with cocoa. Using a 1½-inch heart-shaped cookie cutter, cut the dough into shapes. Place cookies onto a parchment-lined cookie sheet, spacing each 2 inches apart.

5. Bake 12 to 15 minutes or until firm.

6. Remove cookie sheet from the oven. Using a metal spatula, remove cookies from the cookie sheet and place onto a wire cooling rack. Cool completely.

7. Serve plain or dipped or drizzled with chocolate. Store cookies in an airtight container.

YIELD: 50 1½-INCH HEARTS

PEANUT BUTTER BALLS

This recipe is easily doubled or tripled if your family loves them as much as ours does. You may need to finesse the dough texture a bit. It should be firm enough to hold a round shape when rolled. Sometimes the butter or the kitchen itself will be too warm and this will cause the dough to be too soft to hold a firm round shape. If it is too warm, just add a bit more confectioners' sugar until you find the desired texture. If the dough is too dry to roll, add a bit of milk.

We always dip these in dark chocolate, but you can use milk, dark, or white chocolate to coat the treats. The fork drizzle after dipping gives the peanut butter balls a professional look.

4 TABLESPOONS BUTTER, SOFTENED	FOR DIPPING:
½ CUP SMOOTH PEANUT BUTTER	2 CUPS CHOCOLATE CHIPS
1 CUP CONFECTIONERS' SUGAR	1 TABLESPOON VEGETABLE SHORTENING

1. In an electric mixer, cream the butter and peanut butter until smooth. On low speed, add confectioners' sugar. Mix just until blended.

2. Roll dough into ½-inch balls. Place on a parchment-lined cookie sheet, spacing each 1 inch apart. Cover with plastic wrap and freeze overnight.

3. Over simmering water in a double boiler, melt chocolate chips and shortening.

4. Using a fork and spoon, dip peanut butter ball into melted chocolate. Drip off excess chocolate and place dipped ball bottom side down on a parchment-lined cookie sheet. Repeat with remaining balls.

5. Dip fork into melted chocolate. Shake fork back and forth over tops of dipped balls to drizzle. Let dry completely. Store refrigerated in an airtight container.

YIELD: 40 BALLS

AMARETTO CHEESECAKE BROWNIES

Amaretto liqueur and mascarpone cheese combine to give these brownies a touch of Italy. Buon appetito!

BROWNIE:

4 OUNCES CHOCOLATE CHIPS

¼ POUND BUTTER

3 EGGS

2 TEASPOONS AMARETTO

1 CUP SUGAR

¾ CUP FLOUR

TOPPING:

8 OUNCES MASCARPONE CHEESE, SOFTENED

½ CUP SUGAR

2 TEASPOONS AMARETTO

1 EGG

2 TABLESPOONS FLOUR

1. Preheat oven to 350°F.

2. Grease an 8 × 8 × 2-inch baking pan.

3. Over simmering water, or in microwave, melt chocolate chips and butter. Cool.

4. In an electric mixer, on medium speed, beat eggs, amaretto, and sugar. Add chocolate mixture. Mix until smooth. On low speed, add flour. Mix just until blended.

5. Prepare filling. In a another bowl, cream mascarpone and sugar. Add amaretto, egg, and flour. Mix just until blended.

6. Spread two-thirds of the brownie mixture into prepared pan. Pour filling on top of brownie mixture. Dot remaining brownie mixture on top of cheese mixture.

7. Bake 30 to 35 minutes.

8. Remove pan from the oven and place on a wire cooling rack. Cool completely. Refrigerate and cut into squares. Store bars in refrigerator.

YIELD: 20 SQUARES

SUSIE'S CHOCOLATE CHERRY BOMBS

My friend Susie is a fantastic baker. These are just one of her many chocolate specialties. Be sure to use pitted cherries, without stems.

25 WHOLE MARASCHINO CHERRIES, PLUS JUICE (16 OUNCES)

1/4 POUND MARGARINE, SOFTENED

1 CUP SUGAR

1 1/2 CUPS FLOUR

1/2 CUP COCOA

1/2 TEASPOON BAKING SODA

1/4 TEASPOON SALT

1 CUP CHOCOLATE CHIPS

COATING:

1 1/2 CUPS CHOCOLATE CHIPS

1 TABLESPOON SHORTENING

1. Preheat oven to 350°F.

2. Drain cherries and reserve juice. Blot cherries with a paper towel to dry thoroughly. Set aside cherries and juice.

3. In an electric mixer, cream margarine and sugar until light. Add 1/4 cup cherry juice. Mix until well blended. On low speed, add flour, cocoa, baking soda, and salt. Mix just until blended. Stir in chocolate chips.

4. Break off a piece of dough, about a 1 1/2-inch ball. Flatten and insert cherry. Wrap dough around cherry. Roll into a ball about the size of a small golf ball. Be sure the cherry is completely covered. Place on a parchment-lined cookie sheet, spacing each about 2 inches apart.

5. Bake 15 to 20 minutes. Tops will crack. Using a metal spatula, remove cookies from the cookie sheet and place on a wire cooling rack. Cool completely.

6. Melt chocolate chips over simmering water or in microwave. Stir in 1 tablespoon shortening. Frost tops of cookies with chocolate mixture. Allow frosting to set at room temperature. Store in an airtight container.

YIELD: 25 COOKIES

CHOCOLATE CHIP PECAN PIE SQUARES

*This gooey pie bar is almost too decadent to be called a cookie.
You can enjoy these bars served chilled, or slightly
warmed "à la mode" like pecan pie.*

CRUST:

1½ STICKS BUTTER, SOFTENED

¼ CUP SUGAR

1 EGG

2 CUPS FLOUR

FILLING:

4 EGGS

1 CUP SUGAR

½ CUP LIGHT CORN SYRUP

3 TABLESPOONS BUTTER, MELTED

2 CUPS PECAN HALVES

1½ CUPS CHOCOLATE CHIPS

1. Preheat oven to 350°F.

2. Grease a 13 × 9-inch baking pan. Set aside.

3. Prepare crust. In an electric mixer, cream butter and sugar until light. Add egg. Mix well. On low speed, add flour. Mix just until blended. Press dough into prepared pan.

4. Bake 15 to 20 minutes or until lightly browned.

5. Prepare filling. In an electric mixer, beat eggs and sugar. Add corn syrup and butter. Mix well. Stir in pecans and chocolate chips. Pour filling over hot crust.

6. Bake 20 to 25 minutes, or until center is set.

7. Remove pan from the oven. Cool in pan on a wire cooling rack. Cut into squares. Serve with ice cream, if desired.

YIELD: 24 SQUARES

CHOCOLATE APRICOT OAT BARS

The flavor of these bars really comes to life when you toast the wheat germ first. Simply spread the wheat germ on a parchment-lined cookie sheet, and toast in the oven about 12 minutes or until lightly browned. Cool completely before using.

CRUST:

1 ½ CUPS OATS

1 CUP FLOUR

¾ CUP BROWN SUGAR

2 TABLESPOONS WHEAT GERM, TOASTED

¼ TEASPOON BAKING SODA

1 ½ STICKS BUTTER, SOFTENED

FILLING:

¾ CUP APRICOT PRESERVES

¾ CUP CHOCOLATE CHIPS

1. Preheat oven to 350°F.

2. Grease an 8 × 8 × 2-inch baking dish. Set aside.

3. In an electric mixer, combine oats, flour, brown sugar, wheat germ, and baking soda. Mix on low speed. Add butter. Continue to mix on low until mixture is crumbly.

4. Reserve 1 cup of the crumb mixture. Set aside.

5. Press remaining crumb mixture into prepared pan. Spread apricot preserves over the crust. Sprinkle chocolate chips over apricot preserves. Sprinkle with remaining crumb mixture. Press top gently.

6. Bake 20 to 25 minutes, or until golden brown.

7. Remove pan from the oven. Cool cookies in pan on a wire cooling rack. When completely cool, cut into squares. Store in an airtight container.

YIELD: 20 SQUARES

WHITE CHOCOLATE PISTACHIO BARS

These layered bars are an amazing combination of sweet and salty.
For easy cutting, refrigerate before cutting into squares.

1/4 POUND BUTTER

1 1/2 CUPS GRAHAM CRACKER CRUMBS

1 1/2 CUPS COCONUT

1 1/2 CUPS PISTACHIO NUTS

1 1/2 CUPS WHITE CHOCOLATE CHIPS

14 OUNCES SWEETENED CONDENSED MILK

1. Preheat oven to 350°F.

2. Place butter in a 13 × 9-inch baking pan. Place pan in oven to melt butter, about 5 minutes. Remove pan from the oven.

3. Sprinkle graham cracker crumbs on top of melted butter. Spread evenly and press lightly.

4. Spread 1 cup of coconut over the graham cracker crumbs. Reserve ½ cup coconut. Set aside.

5. Sprinkle pistachios on top of coconut. Spread white chocolate chips over pistachios. Using a teaspoon, drizzle sweetened condensed milk over the white chocolate chips. Top with remaining coconut.

6. Bake 25 to 30 minutes or until evenly browned.

7. Remove pan from the oven. Cool pan on a wire cooling rack. Cool completely. Cut into squares and serve. Store in an airtight container.

YIELD: 24 SQUARES

CHOCOLATE BANANA
BOURBON BARS

These moist bars are topped with a rich chocolate ganache topping. Chocolate and banana is a winning combination, especially in these bars.

1½ STICKS BUTTER, SOFTENED	1 TEASPOON BAKING SODA
1 CUP SUGAR	1 TEASPOON BAKING POWDER
2 EGGS	¼ TEASPOON SALT
1 CUP MASHED BANANAS (2 LARGE)	CHOCOLATE GANACHE TOPPING (PAGE 118)
2 TABLESPOONS BOURBON	
2 CUPS FLOUR	

1. Preheat oven to 350°F.

2. Grease a 13 × 9-inch baking pan. Set aside.

3. In an electric mixer, cream butter and sugar until light. Add eggs, bananas, and bourbon. Mix until well blended. On low speed, add flour, baking soda, baking powder, and salt. Mix just until blended. Spread batter evenly in prepared pan.

4. Bake 20 to 25 minutes. Check the center with a toothpick or cake tester. There should be a slight crumb, but it should not be wet in the center.

5. Remove pan from the oven. Place pan on a wire cooling rack. Cool completely. Frost with chocolate ganache topping (see page 118). Store cookies in pan and cut into squares as needed.

YIELD: 24 SQUARES

CHOCOLATE GANACHE TOPPING

This frosting is perfect for all brownies.

1 CUP SEMISWEET CHOCOLATE CHIPS   1 TABLESPOON BUTTER
1/2 CUP HEAVY CREAM

1. In a food processor, pulse chips until finely ground. Place chocolate in a small mixing bowl.

2. In a small saucepan, heat the cream over medium heat. Stirring constantly, bring the cream to a boil. Pour hot cream over chocolate. Stir until chocolate is melted and color is uniform. Stir in butter. Stir until well blended.

3. Spread ganache evenly over the top of chocolate bourbon banana bars. Refrigerate to set. Cut into squares.

CHOCOLATE CHILI PEPPER COOKIES

These chocolate cookies have just a touch of heat, from adding chili powder to the dough. It is an old Mayan custom to combine chocolate with chili—and I was also inspired by the film Chocolat, *which is a chocolate lover's fantasy.*

½ POUND BUTTER, SOFTENED	2 TEASPOONS CHILI POWDER
½ CUP SUGAR	1 ½ CUPS FLOUR
1 TEASPOON VANILLA EXTRACT	⅓ CUP COCOA

1. Preheat oven to 350°F.

2. In an electric mixer on medium speed, cream butter and sugar until light. Add vanilla and chili powder. Mix until well blended.

3. On low speed add flour and cocoa. Mix just until blended.

4. Roll dough into 1-inch balls. If dough is sticky, dust your fingers lightly with cocoa. Place balls on a parchment-lined cookie sheet, spacing each 2 inches apart.

5. Bake 10 to 12 minutes or until firm.

6. Remove cookie sheet from the oven. Using a metal spatula, remove cookies from the cookie sheet and place on a wire cooling rack. Cool completely. Store cookies at room temperature in an airtight container.

YIELD: 24 COOKIES

RICH COFFEE TRUFFLES

These rich little treats are full of the great combination of coffee and chocolate. These are easy to make, a little bit messy, but ideal for chocolate lovers everywhere. They can be served as part of a dessert buffet or wrapped as a take-home treat. I use a small ice cream scoop or melon baller to scoop out truffles to roll.

½ CUP HEAVY CREAM

3 TABLESPOONS BUTTER

1 TABLESPOON LIGHT CORN SYRUP

1½ CUPS CHOCOLATE CHIPS

2 TABLESPOONS COFFEE LIQUEUR

1 TEASPOON INSTANT ESPRESSO POWDER

COCOA FOR COATING

1. In a small saucepan over low heat, combine heavy cream, butter, corn syrup, and chocolate. Heat over low heat, stirring constantly, until butter and chocolate melt and mixture is smooth. Remove from the heat.

2. Stir in coffee liqueur and espresso powder. Stir until blended. Transfer mixture to a bowl. Cover and refrigerate overnight.

3. Roll mixture into ½-inch balls. Roll in cocoa. Place on a parchment-lined tray or plate. If the mixture is sticky, dust your fingers with additional cocoa.

4. Cover truffles with plastic wrap. Refrigerate until serving.

YIELD: 40 TRUFFLES

TOASTED ALMOND WHITE CHOCOLATE TRUFFLES

These white chocolate treats are perfectly accented with toasted almonds and almond liqueur. The name "truffle" comes from the famous fungus with a similar shape—but all you'll think of is their sweet almond flavor when you eat them.

1 ½ CUPS WHITE CHOCOLATE CHIPS

½ CUP HEAVY CREAM

1 CUP ALMONDS, TOASTED AND FINELY CHOPPED

1 TABLESPOON ALMOND LIQUEUR

CONFECFIONERS' SUGAR FOR COATING

1. In a double boiler over simmering water, melt chocolate with heavy cream. Stir to blend well.

2. Remove from the heat. Stir in almonds and almond liqueur. Refrigerate until thick enough to roll into balls, about 3 to 4 hours.

3. Dust fingers with confectioners' sugar. Roll dough into ¾-inch balls. Roll in confectioners' sugar.

4. Place on a parchment-lined cookie sheet. Refrigerate until serving.

YIELD: 30 TRUFFLES

SANDY'S EASY FUDGE

This smooth fudge uses sweetened condensed milk for its sweetness and smoothness. It's an easy-to-make fudge, with no fussy candy thermometers necessary. My friend Sweet Sandy shared this family favorite.

2¼ CUPS CHOCOLATE CHIPS

1 CAN SWEETENED CONDENSED MILK

1 TEASPOON VANILLA EXTRACT

PINCH OF SALT

1 CUP WALNUTS, COARSELY CHOPPED

1. Grease an 8 × 8 × 2-inch baking dish. Set aside.

2. In a double boiler over low heat, melt chocolate chips. Stir constantly until smooth. Remove from the heat. Stir in sweetened condensed milk, vanilla, salt, and walnuts. Mix until blended.

3. Pour into prepared pan and spread evenly. Cover top of pan with plastic wrap and refrigerate until set. Cut into squares. Store fudge, covered, in refrigerator.

YIELD: 20 SQUARES

CHAPTER 5

HOLIDAY FAVORITES

The holidays are always a popular time for baking. No matter how crazy the holiday season may get, people always feel nostalgic for home-baked goods. Whether you're carrying on a family tradition or starting one of your own, baking cookies is a great way to spend time together and treat your family and friends to cookies. Today, when Milanos are made by robots, people will appreciate the time you'll spend creating and baking a special treat. Santa loves when cookies are left for him. Your loved ones will, too.

COOKIE SWAP OR EXCHANGE

You can get together with friends to bake cookies, or schedule a cookie swap or cookie exchange. Not only is this a great way to spend an afternoon or evening with friends, but it also allows you to sample a large variety of cookies—and you'll only have to bake one kind. This is how a swap works: Say you plan the event with ten friends. Each friend bakes 10 dozen of one type of cookie. At the swap, everyone takes one dozen of each type of cookie. Everyone leaves with 10 varieties of cookies. You can also include recipes for the cookies. People are choosing this option not only around the holidays, but before weddings and showers, too. This can also be a popular social event with refreshments and light sandwiches or hors d'oeuvres. I have friends that do an annual "mother-daughter" cookie swap that promotes baking and keeping up relationships. It is a good idea to ask participants what type of cookie they will be bringing. This can avoid having 2 or 3 of the same type of cookie.

GIFT-GIVING IDEAS

You can present a tray of cookies, festively wrapped and tied with a bow, as a great gift. You can also package cookies as gifts in baskets, ceramic planters, tool boxes, or handmade pottery. The container of the cookies can reflect the personality of the receiver. Plus, the recipient will have the plate, planter, or toolbox to reuse. A terrific gift!

SHIPPING COOKIES

The holidays are a good time to ship cookies to friends and relatives. Sturdy cookies work best. You should package the cookies in a tin with a tight-fitting lid. Place the tin in a sturdy crush-proof corrugated box. Cushion around the tin with crumpled newspaper and tissue paper. Ship the quickest method, either overnight or second-day service. Mark the box "perishable." This way the recipient will be sure to know to open it right away. This is especially important if they're not expecting a package of treats.

PUMPKIN PIE DROPS

*These moist drops are a perfect addition to your
Thanksgiving traditions. In fact, they'd be
welcome at any autumn gathering.*

½ POUND BUTTER, SOFTENED	1 TEASPOON BAKING SODA
1 CUP BROWN SUGAR	1 TEASPOON CINNAMON
1 EGG	¼ TEASPOON NUTMEG
1 CUP CANNED PUMPKIN	¼ TEASPOON CLOVES
2 CUPS FLOUR	CINNAMON CONFECTONERS' ICING (PAGE 126)

1. Preheat oven to 350°F.

2. In an electric mixer, on medium speed, cream butter and brown sugar until light. Add egg and pumpkin. Mix until well blended.

3. On low speed, add flour, baking soda, cinnamon, nutmeg, and cloves. Mix just until blended.

4. Drop dough from a teaspoon onto a parchment-lined cookie sheet, spacing each 2 inches apart.

5. Bake 10 to 12 minutes, or until firm.

6. Remove cookie sheet from the oven. Using a metal spatula, remove cookies from the cookie sheet and place on a wire cooling rack. Cool completely.

7. Frost with cinnamon confectioners' icing (see page 126). Place a wire cooling rack on top of a parchment-lined cookie sheet. This will catch any excess frosting and will make cleanup easier. Using a small spatula or butter knife, frost the top of the cookie. You don't have to frost the entire surface of the cookie. The frosting will naturally fall down the sides of the cookie.

8. Let frosting dry completely. Store in an airtight container at room temperature.

YIELD: 50 COOKIES

CINNAMON CONFECTIONERS' ICING

3 CUPS CONFECTIONERS' SUGAR　　　**½ CUP WATER**
1 TEASPOON CINNAMON

In an electric mixer, combine all ingredients. Mix until well blended and smooth.

GINGERBREAD COOKIES

This versatile dough can be used to make cookies or gingerbread houses. It is functional and delicious, especially for the holidays. At Sweet Maria's we make an equal amount of ginger men and ginger women. The women are always more fun to decorate, with flowers in their hair and lacy skirts.

1/2 POUND MARGARINE, SOFTENED	1 1/2 TEASPOONS GINGER
1 1/2 CUPS SUGAR	1 1/2 TEASPOONS CINNAMON
2 EGGS	3 TEASPOONS BAKING SODA
1/2 CUP MOLASSES	3 1/2 CUPS FLOUR

1. In an electric mixer, cream margarine and sugar until light. Add eggs and molasses. Mix until well blended. Add ginger, cinnamon, baking soda, and flour. Mix on low speed just until blended. Wrap dough in plastic and refrigerate overnight.

2. Preheat oven to 350°F.

3. Roll dough out onto a lightly floured surface, about 1/8-inch thick. Using a cookie cutter, cut dough into desired shapes. Place cookies onto a parchment-lined cookie sheet, spacing each about 2 inches apart.

4. Bake 8 to 10 minutes or until evenly browned.

5. Remove cookie sheet from the oven. Using a metal spatula, remove cookies from the cookie sheet and place on a wire cooling rack. Cool completely.

6. Decorate, if desired, with cookie decorating frosting (see page 128), using a pastry bag fitted with tip #5 (large writing tip). For small details, use tip #3.

YIELD: ABOUT 40 FLOWER COOKIES (3-INCH FLOWER CUTTER)
OR 20 GINGERPEOPLE (6 INCHES TALL)

COOKIE DECORATING FROSTING

This frosting is used to decorate gingerbread cookies, sour cream cutouts, and other sugar cookies. It is also called royal icing, and it will air-dry overnight. This makes it the ideal frosting to use when making cookies for individually wrapped gifts. After the icing dries, wrap your creations in cellophane bags and tie with a festive ribbon.

This icing is very flexible. You can add whatever extract and/or food colorings you prefer. There is also flexibility in its texture. To decorate cookies piped from a pastry bag or to assemble a gingerbread house, the frosting needs to be stiff. You may need to add more confectioners' sugar. To get a smooth, glossy surface on a cookie, water must be added to make a soft frosting. Do not refrigerate cookies decorated with this frosting. The frosting will melt. Let frosted cookies air-dry and store in airtight containers at room temperature.

4 CUPS CONFECTIONERS' SUGAR

1/2 TEASPOON LEMON EXTRACT (OR OTHER FLAVORING)

3 TABLESPOONS WATER

1/2 TEASPOON CREAM OF TARTAR

2 EGG WHITES

FOOD COLORING (OPTIONAL)

Combine all ingredients in an electric mixer. Mix on low speed until blended. Whip on high speed 2 to 3 minutes or until shiny and smooth. Add food coloring, if desired. Store in an airtight container.

YIELD: ABOUT 2 CUPS

ORANGE PFEFFERNÜSSE

*A new twist on an old holiday favorite, these "pepper balls"
have a zesty orange flavor. This German favorite is a
great cookie with which to celebrate the season.*

2½ CUPS FLOUR

½ TEASPOON BAKING SODA

½ TEASPOON SALT

¼ TEASPOON BLACK PEPPER

½ TEASPOON BAKING POWDER

1 TEASPOON CINNAMON

1 CUP HONEY

1 EGG

GRATED RIND OF ONE ORANGE

4 TABLESPOONS BUTTER, MELTED AND
COOLED

CONFECTIONERS' SUGAR FOR
COATING

1. Preheat oven to 350°F.

2. In a medium bowl, combine flour, baking soda, salt, black pepper, baking powder, and cinnamon. With a wooden spoon, mix until blended.

3. Add honey, egg, rind, and butter. Stir until well blended.

4. Roll dough into 1-inch balls and place on a parchment-lined cookie sheet, spacing each 2 inches apart.

5. Bake 12 to 15 minutes or until golden brown.

6. Remove cookie sheet from the oven. Carefully roll warm cookies in confectioners sugar. Cool completely.

YIELD: 40 COOKIES

FRUITCAKE SQUARES

Forget all the old jokes about fruitcake. These colorful and tasty bars are an easy way to brighten up a holiday table. Be sure to use a combination of red and green cherries for the fullest color. You can also substitute holiday favorites such as citron or candied pineapple.

1 ½ STICKS BUTTER, SOFTENED

1 CUP SUGAR

1 TEASPOON VANILLA EXTRACT

4 EGGS

1 ¼ CUPS FLOUR

2 CUPS GLACÉ CHERRIES
(RED AND GREEN)

2 CUPS CHOPPED WALNUTS

CONFECTIONERS' SUGAR FOR
DUSTING

1. Preheat oven to 350°F.

2. Grease a 13 × 9-inch baking pan.

3. In an electric mixer on medium speed, cream butter and sugar until light. Add vanilla and eggs. Mix until well blended. On low speed, add flour, cherries, and nuts. Spread dough into prepared pan.

5. Bake 25 to 30 minutes or until lightly browned.

6. Remove pan from the oven. Let cool completely on a wire cooling rack.

7. Dust with confectioners' sugar. Cut into squares. Store in an airtight container at room temperature.

YIELD: 24 SQUARES

THUMBPRINT COOKIES

Nothing says home-baked like these jelly-filled cookies. Roll them in coconut or chopped walnuts and fill them with your favorite flavors. Mine is plum, from our very own plum tree.

½ POUND BUTTER, SOFTENED

½ CUP SUGAR

2 EGGS, SEPARATED

2 TEASPOONS VANILLA EXTRACT

2 CUPS FLOUR

½ TEASPOON SALT

2 CUPS FINELY CHOPPED WALNUTS OR COCONUT

¾ CUP JELLY

1. Preheat oven to 350°F.

2. In an electric mixer, cream the butter and sugar until light. Add the egg yolks and vanilla. Mix until well blended. On low speed, gradually add flour and salt. Mix just until blended to form a soft dough.

3. Roll dough into 1-inch balls.

4. In a small bowl, beat egg whites with a fork until fluffy. Place chopped nuts or coconut in another small bowl.

5. Dip balls into egg whites and then roll in nuts (or coconut). Coat thoroughly. Place balls on a parchment-lined cookie sheet, spacing each 2 inches apart.

6. Using your fingers, press the tops of the balls to flatten slightly. With your index finger, make a hole in the center of each cookie.

7. Spoon ½ teaspoon of jelly into each hole.

8. Bake for 15 to 20 minutes, or until lightly browned.

9. Remove cookie sheet from the oven. Using a metal spatula, remove cookies and place on a wire cooling rack. Cool. Store in an airtight container.

YIELD: 35 COOKIES

CINNAMON LACE COOKIES

These are crispy, flavorful cookies. I love them plain or sandwiched together with melted chocolate.

1 ½ CUPS CHOPPED WALNUTS	½ STICK BUTTER
½ CUP FLOUR	¾ CUP SUGAR
½ TEASPOON CINNAMON	¾ CUP HEAVY CREAM

1. Preheat oven to 350°F.

2. In a medium bowl, combine walnuts, flour, and cinnamon. Set aside.

3. In a small saucepan, on medium heat, combine butter, sugar, and heavy cream. Stir until butter melts and mixture comes to a boil. Pour over dry ingredients. Stir until well blended. Let cool slightly.

4. Using a heaping teaspoon, drop dough onto a parchment-lined cookie sheet, 4 inches apart. Using the back of the teaspoon, spread into 2-inch-diameter circles.

5. Bake 10 to 12 minutes or until edges begin to brown.

6. Remove cookie sheet from the oven. Using a metal spatula, remove cookies from the cookie sheet and place on a wire cooling rack. Cool completely. Store cookies in an airtight container.

YIELD: 30 COOKIES

◆ LACE COOKIE DESSERTS ◆

TO MAKE AN IMPRESSIVE DESSERT, SANDWICH TWO OR THREE LACE COOKIES WITH WHIPPED CREAM AND SLICED STRAWBERRIES IN BETWEEN. THIS WILL MAKE THE PERFECT FINALE TO ANY MEAL.

CRANBERRY APRICOT COCONUT BALLS

These brightly colored no-bake treats are a pretty addition to cookie trays and delicious to eat. They're another simple, no-bake cookie that's perfect for today's busy lifestyle.

1 CUP DRIED CRANBERRIES, CHOPPED   1 1/2 CUPS COCONUT, TOASTED

1 CUP DRIED APRICOTS, CHOPPED   2/3 CUP SWEETENED CONDENSED MILK

1. In a medium bowl, combine cranberries, apricots, and 1/2 cup coconut. With a wooden spoon, mix until well blended. Stir in condensed milk. Refrigerate dough 1 hour.

2. Remove dough from the refrigerator. Roll dough into 1/2-inch balls. Dough may be sticky. Dip fingers in water so that dough does not stick to hands. Roll balls in remaining coconut. Place on a parchment-lined cookie sheet. Refrigerate until serving.

3. Store cookies in an airtight container in refrigerator.

YIELD: 30 COOKIES

♦ HOW TO TOAST COCONUT ♦

TO TOAST COCONUT, SPREAD A THIN LAYER OF COCONUT ON A PARCHMENT-LINED COOKIE SHEET. BAKE AT 350° 10 TO 12 MINUTES, STIRRING OCCASIONALLY, TO TOAST UNTIL LIGHTLY BROWNED. LET COOL BEFORE USING.

GUMDROP COOKIES

*Colorful gumdrop cookies are perfect for all your holiday cookie trays.
Kids especially love to make and eat them. For a tasty variation,
substitute 2½ cups M&M candies instead of the gumdrops.
They'll be festive and delicious either way.*

½ POUND BUTTER, SOFTENED	2 CUPS FLOUR
1 CUP SUGAR	½ TEASPOON BAKING SODA
1 TEASPOON VANILLA EXTRACT	2 CUPS GUMDROPS
2 EGGS	

1. Preheat oven to 350°F.

2. In an electric mixer, cream butter and sugar until light. Add vanilla and eggs. Mix until well blended. On low speed, add flour and baking soda. Mix just until blended. Stir in gumdrops.

3. Drop dough from a teaspoon onto a parchment-lined cookie sheet, spacing each 2 inches apart.

4. Bake 12 to 15 minutes or until edges begin to brown.

5. Remove cookie sheet from the oven. Using a metal spatula, remove cookies from the cookie sheet and place on a wire cooling rack. Cool.

6. Store cookies in an airtight container at room temperature.

YIELD: 40 COOKIES

WREATH COOKIES

These cookies are great to bake with kids. They'll love to decorate them
with colored coconut and cherries. You can also make a variation
for Easter that forms the dough into Easter baskets.

¼ POUND BUTTER, SOFTENED

½ CUP SUGAR

1 TEASPOON VANILLA EXTRACT

1 EGG

2 CUPS FLOUR

½ CUP MARASCHINO CHERRIES, CHOPPED

½ CUP COCONUT

1. Preheat oven to 350°F.

2. In an electric mixer, cream butter and sugar until light. Add vanilla and egg.
   Mix until well blended. On low speed, add flour. Mix just until blended. Stir in
   cherries and coconut.

3. Break off a piece of dough. Roll on a lightly floured surface into a pencil-thick
   strip about 6 inches long. Form strip into a ring and press edges together to
   seal. Roll and shape remaining dough. Place rings onto a parchment-lined
   cookie sheet, spacing each 2 inches apart.

4. Bake 12 to 15 minutes or until lightly browned.

5. Remove baking sheet from the oven. Using a metal spatula, remove cookies
   from the cookie sheet and place on a wire cooling rack. Cool completely, frost,
   and decorate (see page 136).

YIELD: 30 COOKIES

WREATH FROSTING

2 CUPS CONFECTIONERS' SUGAR

¼ CUP OR A BIT LESS WATER

1 TO 1½ CUPS COCONUT, COLORED GREEN

ABOUT 30 PIECES OF CHOPPED GLACÉ CHERRIES

Mix confectioners' sugar with water until smooth. Frost tops of cookie with wreath frosting. While frosting is still wet, sprinkle with green coconut and glacé cherries, as desired. Let dry completely. Store cookies in an airtight container.

VARIATION: EASTER BASKETS

Make tighter rings while shaping dough so that there is a smaller hole. Frost cookies with wreath frosting. Sprinkle with green coconut and place jelly beans in frosting. Let dry. Store cookies in an airtight container.

◆ HOW TO COLOR COCONUT ◆

PLACE 2 CUPS OF COCONUT IN A MEDIUM BOWL. ADD 2 TO 3 DROPS OF LIQUID FOOD COLORING. TOSS WITH YOUR FINGERS OR A WOODEN SPOON TO ACHIEVE DESIRED COLOR. IT'S ALWAYS EASIER TO START WITH LESS COLOR AND GRADUALLY ADD MORE. IF YOU'RE USING PASTE FOOD COLORS, ADD WATER TO PASTE COLOR, THEN ADD TO COCONUT.

DATE NUT BALLS

*These are delicious no-bake cookies that use Rice Krispies cereal for a
crunchy partner to dates and walnuts. This recipe can be easily doubled.
Make a double batch, and share some with your Secret Santa.*

¼ POUND BUTTER	1 CUP DATES, CHOPPED
½ CUP SUGAR	2 CUPS PUFFED RICE CEREAL
1 TEASPOON VANILLA EXTRACT	1 CUP WALNUTS, FINELY CHOPPED
1 EGG	

1. In a medium saucepan over medium low heat, melt butter. Add sugar, vanilla,
   egg, and dates. Stir constantly 3 to 4 minutes or until egg is cooked and mixture
   is slightly thickened.

2. Remove pan from the heat. Stir in puffed rice cereal and walnuts. Mix until well
   blended. Set aside to cool.

3. When cool, roll into 1-inch balls. If dough is sticky, dip fingers in water and
   then roll. Place cookies on a parchment-lined cookie sheet. Refrigerate until
   serving. Store cookies in an airtight container in refrigerator.

YIELD: 30 COOKIES

AUNT BABE'S PECAN TASSIES

These little nut tarts are a special treat for any occasion. They can be a bit labor intensive, so be sure to savor every bite when someone gives you a tray of tassies. Press the dough into a miniature muffin pan to form the crust. A tart shaper can be used to form crust into the pan (these are available at most kitchen shops). If you have only one pan, be sure to let it cool before filling it again.

CRUST:

3 OUNCES CREAM CHEESE, ROOM TEMPERATURE

¼ POUND BUTTER, SOFTENED

1 CUP FLOUR

FILLING:

1 EGG

¾ CUP BROWN SUGAR

1 TABLESPOON BUTTER, MELTED AND COOLED

½ TEASPOON VANILLA EXTRACT

¼ CUP PECANS, FINELY CHOPPED

24 PECAN HALVES

1. Prepare crust. In an electric mixer, cream cream cheese and butter until fluffy. On low speed, add flour. Mix just until blended. Wrap dough in plastic wrap and refrigerate 2 to 3 hours or overnight.

2. Preheat oven to 350°F.

3. Prepare filling. In a medium mixing bowl, beat egg, brown sugar, butter, and vanilla. Mix until well blended. Stir in chopped pecans. Set aside.

4. Roll dough into 1-inch balls. Press ball into a greased mini muffin pan. Line pan on the bottom and sides. Using a teaspoon, fill the muffin cups with filling. Top with pecan half.

5. Bake 20 to 25 minutes or until edges begin to brown.

6. Remove pan from the oven. Cool in pan on a wire rack. Repeat with remaining dough and filling. Store in an airtight container.

YIELD: 24 TASSIES

VARIATION:

LEMON PISTACHIO TASSIES

This variation uses the same crust as the pecan tassies, but has a zesty lemon filling containing pistachios.

FILLING:

1 EGG

¾ CUP SUGAR

1 TABLESPOON BUTTER, MELTED AND COOLED

GRATED RIND OF 1 LEMON

½ CUP PISTACHIOS, FINELY CHOPPED

Follow same directions as for making Pecan Tassies.

EGGNOG COOKIES

These moist and simple drop cookies really capture the flavor of Christmas. After frosting, be sure to sprinkle the tops with nutmeg while the frosting is still wet.

¼ POUND BUTTER, SOFTENED	1 ½ CUPS FLOUR
½ CUP SUGAR	½ TEASPOON BAKING POWDER
1 EGG	½ TEASPOON SODA
½ CUP EGGNOG	PINCH OF SALT
	EGGNOG FROSTING (PAGE 141)

1. Preheat oven to 350°F.

2. In an electric mixer, cream butter and sugar until light. Add egg and eggnog. Mix until well blended. On low speed, add flour, baking powder, baking soda, and salt. Mix just until blended. Dough will be soft and a little sticky.

3. Drop dough from a teaspoon onto a parchment-lined cookie sheet, spacing each 2 inches apart.

4. Bake 10 to 12 minutes or until edges begin to brown.

5. Remove cookie sheet from the oven. Using a metal spatula, remove cookies from the sheet and place on a wire cooling rack. Cool completely. Frost with eggnog frosting (page 141). Sprinkle with nutmeg.

YIELD: 36 COOKIES

EGGNOG FROSTING

This frosting is the perfect accent for the eggnog cookies.

3 CUPS CONFECTIONERS' SUGAR

¼ CUP PLUS 2 TABLESPOONS EGGNOG

3 TABLESPOONS RUM

1. In an electric mixer, combine all ingredients. Mix until smooth.

2. Place a wire cooling rack on top of a parchment-lined cookie sheet. This will catch any excess frosting and will make cleanup easier. Using a metal spatula, frost the top of the cookies. Frosting will drizzle down the cookies. Sprinkle tops with nutmeg. Let dry.

PERSIMMON COOKIES

*These tasty spice cookies have the unique addition of pureed persimmon.
A popular fruit found at the holiday table, served in a fruit assortment
or in holiday desserts, persimmons are a sure sign that autumn has
arrived. Persimmons need to be completely soft before using.
To puree the persimmon, remove skin and cut into cubes. Pulse
in food processor 1 to 2 minutes.*

¼ POUND BUTTER, SOFTENED	½ TEASPOON BAKING POWDER
1 CUP BROWN SUGAR	¼ TEASPOON SALT
1 EGG	1 TEASPOON CINNAMON
1 TEASPOON VANILLA EXTRACT	1 CUP PURÉED PERSIMMON
1½ CUPS FLOUR	1 CUP WALNUTS, CHOPPED
½ TEASPOON BAKING SODA	

1. Preheat oven to 350°F.

2. In an electric mixer, cream butter and brown sugar until light. Add egg and vanilla. Mix well. On low speed, add flour, baking soda, baking powder, salt, and cinnamon. Mix just until blended. Stir in persimmon and walnuts.

3. Drop from a rounded teaspoon onto a parchment-lined cookie sheet, spacing each 2 inches apart.

4. Bake 10 to 12 minutes, or until firm.

5. Remove cookie sheet from the oven. Using a metal spatula, remove cookies from the cookie sheet and place on a wire cooling rack. Cool completely. Store cookies in an airtight container.

YIELD: 45 COOKIES

CHAPTER 6

LOW-FAT, LOW-SUGAR, AND GLUTEN-FREE COOKIES

This section addresses the special dietary needs of cookie lovers. For what they may lack in fat, sugar, or gluten, these cookies certainly aren't lacking in flavor.

Low fat: Our low-fat cookies use egg whites and sugar and include the meringues in this chapter. Other low-fat recipes in this book are Pignoli and Chocolate Almond Macaroons.

Low sugar: Low-sugar cookies use apples and plum purées for a natural sugar that is easy to absorb and a healthy portion of oats.

Gluten free: Those who are allergic to gluten can enjoy my Pignoli or Chocolate Almond Macaroons, Lemon Coconut Macaroons, and Peanut Butter Balls—in addition to the gluten-free cookies in this chapter. This chapter also includes a tasty dog biscuit. After all, *everyone* loves cookies.

APRICOT DATE OATMEAL CHEWS

These chewy, low-fat cookies are moist and tasty, thanks to applesauce and a healthy combination of dried apricots, dates, and oatmeal.

¼ POUND MARGARINE, SOFTENED

½ CUP BROWN SUGAR

2 EGG WHITES

½ CUP APPLESAUCE

1½ CUPS FLOUR

1 TEASPOON BAKING SODA

¼ TEASPOON SALT

2½ CUPS OATS

1 CUP DRIED APRICOTS, COARSELY CHOPPED

1 CUP DATES, COARSELY CHOPPED

1. Preheat oven to 350°F.

2. In an electric mixer, cream margarine and brown sugar until light. Add egg whites and applesauce. Mix until well blended. On low speed, add flour, baking soda, and salt. Mix just until blended. Stir in oats, apricots, and dates.

3. Drop dough from a teaspoon onto a parchment-lined cookie sheet, spacing each 2 inches apart.

4. Bake 12 to 15 minutes, or until lightly browned.

5. Remove cookie sheet from the oven. Using a metal spatula, remove cookies from the cookie sheet and place on a wire cooling rack. Cool. Store cookies at room temperature in an airtight container.

YIELD: 55 COOKIES

CHOCOLATE CLOVE
LESS-FAT COOKIES

This spicy chocolate cookie is the perfect treat
for the low-fat crowd. It'll satisfy anyone's craving
for a chewy chocolate cookie.

1 ¼ CUPS FLOUR	½ TEASPOON SALT
½ CUP SUGAR	½ TEASPOON CLOVES
½ CUP COCOA	½ CUP LIGHT CORN SYRUP
½ TEASPOON BAKING SODA	3 EGG WHITES

1. Preheat oven to 350°F.

2. In an electric mixer, combine flour, sugar, cocoa, baking soda, salt, and cloves. Mix until uniform. Add corn syrup and egg whites. Mix just until blended. Dough will be sticky. Drop dough from a teaspoon onto a parchment-lined cookie sheet, spacing each 2 inches apart.

3. Bake 8 to 10 minutes or until set. Do not overbake.

4. Remove cookie sheet from the oven. Cool cookies completely on parchment. Store cookies in an airtight container.

YIELD: 30 COOKIES

WINTER AND
SUMMER MERINGUES

These cookies are the perfect treat for anyone who has a gluten allergy.
Here are two variations, Lime for a spring and summer treat, or
Maple Spice for cold weather. This recipe uses a pastry bag, without a tip,
to form the dough into small kisses. If you don't want to use a pastry bag,
you can spoon the dough onto the cookie sheet.

LIME MERINGUES

Clean the whip well so that all the grated rind is added to the batter.

4 EGG WHITES	GRATED RIND OF 2 LIMES
1 ¼ CUPS SUGAR	JUICE OF 2 LIMES

1. Preheat oven to 225°F.

2. In an electric mixer, with wire whip, beat egg whites at high speed. Gradually add sugar in a steady stream as you beat egg whites. Add grated rind and juice. Beat until stiff and glossy, about 5 minutes.

3. Using a pastry bag, pipe small kisses onto a parchment-lined cookie sheet. You can pipe cookies close together because they won't spread.

4. Bake 1½ hours or until dry.

5. Remove cookie sheet from the oven. Cool cookies completely on parchment. Store cookies in an airtight container.

YIELD: 70 SMALL MERINGUES

MAPLE SPICE MERINGUES

*A spicy combination of maple and cinnamon make these
cookies a cold-weather treat. Perfect by the
fire with a steaming hot cocoa.*

4 EGG WHITES	1 TEASPOON MAPLE EXTRACT
1 CUP SUGAR	1 TEASPOON CINNAMON

1. Preheat oven to 225°F.

2. In an electric mixer, with wire whip, beat egg whites at high speed. Gradually add sugar as you beat the egg whites. Add maple extract and cinnamon. Beat until stiff and glossy, about 5 minutes.

3. Using a pastry bag, pipe small kisses onto a parchment-lined cookie sheet. You can pipe them close together because they won't spread.

4. Bake 1½ hours or until dry.

5. Remove cookie sheet from the oven. Cool cookies completely on parchment. Store cookies in an airtight container.

YIELD: 70 SMALL MERINGUES

CASHEW CHEWIES

*This cookie is a delicious treat made with simple cashew butter.
I almost hate to categorize it—although the recipe is
gluten free, this cookie is yummy
for anyone to enjoy.*

2 CUPS WHOLE CASHEWS

¼ CUP VEGETABLE OIL

1 CUP BROWN SUGAR

1 EGG

1 TEASPOON VANILLA EXTRACT

1. Preheat oven to 350°F.

2. In a food processor, grind cashews until fine. Add oil in a slow stream while grinding, to form a paste similar in texture to chunky peanut butter. This should yield one cup of cashew butter.

3. In an electric mixer, cream cashew butter and brown sugar. Add egg and vanilla and mix until well blended.

4. Drop dough from a teaspoon onto a parchment-lined cookie sheet, spacing each 2 inches apart.

5. Bake 10 to 12 minutes or until browned.

6. Remove cookie sheet from the oven. Let cookies cool completely on parchment paper. After cooling, remove cookies from the cookie sheet, using a metal spatula. Store cookies in an airtight container.

YIELD: 24 COOKIES

APPLE CINNAMON SUGAR FREES

A chunky, chewy cookie loaded with flavor,
this recipe uses apples and raisins as a natural sweetener.

1½ CUPS RAISINS	1 TEASPOON CINNAMON
¾ CUP APPLE, CHOPPED	1 TEASPOON VANILLA EXTRACT
1 CUP WATER	2 EGGS, BEATEN
½ CUP BUTTER	1 CUP OATS
1 CUP FLOUR	½ CUP WALNUTS, FINELY CHOPPED
1 TEASPOON BAKING SODA	

1. In a medium saucepan, combine raisins, apple, and water. Bring to a boil, over medium heat, and boil 3 to 4 minutes. Remove saucepan from the heat. Stir in butter until melted. Set aside to cool.

2. In a medium mixing bowl, combine flour, baking soda, and cinnamon. Mix until blended. Add vanilla, eggs, oats, walnuts, and cooled raisin mixture. Stir until blended. Cover bowl and refrigerate overnight.

3. Preheat oven to 350°F.

4. Drop dough from a teaspoon onto a parchment-lined cookie sheet, spacing each 2 inches apart.

5. Bake 10 to 12 minutes, or until lightly browned.

6. Remove cookie sheet from the oven. Using a metal spatula, remove cookies from the cookie sheet and place on a wire cooling rack. Cool completely. Store cookies in an airtight container.

YIELD: 45 COOKIES

BOW WOW BISCUITS

Labs, pugs, and shepherds agree—these treats are really yummy.
This newest addition to our Sweet Maria menu keeps them
howling for more. We've tried to make these biscuits various shapes
but found the traditional dog bone shape to be the
easiest for most dogs to eat.

2 BOUILLON CUBES, CHICKEN OR BEEF

1/4 POUND MARGARINE, CUT INTO CUBES

1 EGG, SLIGHTLY BEATEN

2 TEASPOONS SUGAR

1/2 CUP POWDERED MILK

3 TO 3 1/2 CUPS WHOLE WHEAT FLOUR

1/2 TEASPOON SALT

1. Preheat oven to 350°F.

2. Dissolve bouillon cubes in 1 cup of boiling water. Place margarine in a large mixing bowl. Pour hot dissolved bouillon over margarine. Stir to melt margarine. Add egg, sugar, powdered milk, 3 cups flour, and salt. Mix until blended.

3. Turn dough out onto a lightly floured surface. Knead in remaining 1/2 cup flour to make a firm, not sticky dough.

4. Roll dough to 1/2 inch thick. Cut into shapes. Place on a parchment-lined cookie sheet. You can place them close together. They won't spread.

5. Bake 35 to 40 minutes, or until browned and dry. Remove cookie sheet from the oven. Using a metal spatula, remove cookies from the cookie sheet and place on a wire cooling rack. Cool completely.

6. Store biscuits in an airtight container at room temperature.

YIELD: 20 DOG BONE–SHAPE BISCUITS (4 1/2 INCHES LONG)

LIST OF COOKIES
BY METHOD

BAR COOKIES

Almond Triangles, 102

Amaretto Cheesecake Brownies, 112

Brass City Bars, 100

Cheesecake Squares, 101

Chocolate Apricot Oat Bars, 115

Chocolate Banana Bourbon Bars, 117

Chocolate Chip Pecan Blondies, 108

Chocolate Chip Pecan Pie Squares, 114

Cranberry Cobbler Bars, 28

Fluffer Nutter Bars, 33

Fruitcake Squares, 130

Fudge Brownies, 105

Key West Lime Bars, 31

Lemon Poppy Bars, 84

Magic Bars, 21

Prune Bars, 98

Toffee Bars, 106

White Chocolate Pistachio Bars, 116

BISCOTTI

Amaretto Biscotti with Almonds, 63

Chocolate Orange Biscotti, 109

Dried Cherry and Almond Biscotti, 64

DROP COOKIES

Apple Cinnamon Sugar Frees, 150

Apricot Date Oatmeal Chews, 145

Butterscotch Drops, 23

Cappuccino Drops, 97

Cashew Chewies, 149

Chocolate Chip Cookies, 14

Chocolate Chocolate Chip Cookies, 19

Chocolate Clove Less-Fat Cookies, 146

Cinnamon Lace Cookies, 132

Eggnog Cookies, 140

Granola Cookie Drops, 29

Gumdrop Cookies, 134

Italian Drop Cookies, 59

Lemon Coconut Macaroons, 75

Lynn's Sour Cream Sunshine Cookies, 32

Maple Walnut Drops, 24

Oatmeal Raisin Cookies, 18

Persimmon Drops, 142

Piña Colada Cookies, 27

Pumpkin Pie Drops, 125

Swedish Spice Cookies, 39

White Chocolate Chip Cookies, 15

SOURCES

Here are a few of my favorite places to find baking equipment, utensils, and ingredients.

Martha by Mail
1-800-950-7130
www.marthastewart.com
Baking and decorating equipment,
packaging supplies

The Bakers Catalogue
1-800-827-6836
www.bakerscatalogue.com
Equipment, utensils, ingredients

Sur La Table
1-800-243-0852
www.surlatable.com
Equipment and utensils

William-Sonoma
1-800-541-2233
www.williams-sonoma.com
(stores nationwide)
Baking equipment, utensils,
some ingredients

New York Cake and Baking Distributor
56 West 22nd Street
New York, New York 10010
1-800-94-CAKE-9
Equipment, ingredients, utensils

INDEX